HARLEY JAMES AND THE PUZZLE IN PARIS

LEAH CUPPS

Copyright © 2022 Leah Cupps & Vision Forty Press

Harley James Adventures® is a Trademark of Leah Cupps.

www.HarleyJamesAdventures.com

All rights reserved.

No part of this book may be reproduced in any form or by any electronic or mechanical means, including information storage and retrieval systems, without written permission from the author, except for the use of brief quotations in a book review.

ISBN: 978-1-7344055-9-0

NOTE: While inspired by real events, this is a work of fiction and does not claim to be historically accurate or portray factual events or relationships. References to historical events, real persons, business establishments and real places are used fictitiously and my not be factually accurate, but rather fictionalized by the author.

Dedicated to my daughter, Savannah Cupps.

Her curiosity, adventurous spirit and love of dogs inspired the Harley James books.

FREE ACTIVITY KIT

Dear Friend,

Welcome! My name is Harley James and this is my story, the Puzzle in Paris. I'm so glad you're here!

If you love riddles and puzzles as much as I do, then you must download the free activity kit I made, just for you! It includes mazes, puzzles and of course, secret messages!

Go to HarleyJamesAdventures.com to download this fun activity kit for free!

Until then, Happy Reading!

Harley James

P.S. Some of the characters & history in this story is fictional, and some is true. Want to know what's what?

Go to HarleyJamesAdventures.com and click on our free Fact or Fiction Video Series to find out more.

www.HarleyJamesAdventures.com

CONTENTS

Prologue	1
1. The Possibilities of Paris	5
2. Bubbling with Curiosity	10
3. Tower of Trouble?	16
4. Beneath the Surface	22
5. Getting Up to Speed	26
6. An Unexpected Visitor	31
7. The Key to the Plan	36
8. Musée des Plans-Reliefs	40
9. Read Between the Lines	48
10. Legends of the Catacombs	54
11. Home Not-So-Sweet Home	59
12. A Troubled Past	66
13. Preserve, Protect, Persevere	71
14. Spilling the Beans	74
15. High Stakes and Stomachaches	77
16. Small Solutions and Big Problems	81
17. No Way Out	86
18. The Writing on the Wall	92
19. A Close Call	97
20. When Puzzles Cause Problems	104
21. The Hidden Chamber	110
22. A Bright New Day	116
About the Author	121

PROLOGUE

P*aris, France, January 2, 1979*

"Mommy, I'm scared," cried the young girl as she tugged on her mother's sleeve.

"Come on, darling, there's nothing to be afraid of. Just a few more minutes, and we will go get macaroons."

The girl nodded and tried to focus her mind on cookies and not the walls of bones staring out at her.

The family had decided on a tour of the Catacombs of Paris that day. The little girl didn't want to go, but her father insisted. He said the 180 miles of tunnels underneath Paris were one of the modern wonders of the world. They didn't want to miss their chance to see them, did they?

Just as the girl began to tug again at her mother's sleeve, her red scarf caught in the wind. It fluttered away from her and into the tunnels.

The scarf wove its way further into the Catacombs on a bizarre stream of inter-tunnel wind currents. It made its way down, down, down through the underground passages and chambers. Eventually it came to rest at the feet of another young girl with long, dark hair and bright green eyes. She picked up the scarf and wrapped it around her neck appreciatively as she followed her family deeper and deeper into the Catacombs.

"Come, Claudine, hurry now! We cannot be late," the girl's mother called to her in French as they made their way quickly through the maze.

They finally emerged in a chamber located at the end of the maze, reached by way of many secret entrances hidden throughout the city of Paris. Here, a meeting was about to begin. Members of the oldest families in all of France had come together to make a very important decision. One that, if made incorrectly, could start the beginning of the end of the world.

In that dark, echoing room, where no one else could possibly follow or find them without the aid of a secret map, these families had gathered to discuss the matter at hand. The white and gray walls surrounding them were inlaid with a series of tombs and bones to mark the graves where generations of their ancestors had been laid to rest. On the opposite side of the chamber stood a metal doorway that remained tightly sealed.

A man named Jacques Guillaume separated himself from the crowd and stood at the top of the short stone stairwell leading out of the room. He addressed the rest of the families, holding a peculiar item in his hands.

"Families of France, I thank you for coming. This is not a decision to be made alone," he called out. "In the wrong hands, the Rose de France has the power to wreak immense havoc and destruction." He gently raised the item in his shaking hands, almost as though he were afraid to reveal it.

Those present gazed at the glistening, spherical stone about the size of the man's fist. Deep purple veins ran through it and vaporized into a purple glow once it left stone. It might look like a large amethyst gem to the outside world. But here, in this room deep inside the Catacombs, the purple veins came aglow with an unsettling life of their own.

"It cannot stay here," Jacques continued dramatically. "If it were to be in this very room on the day when the right family bloodline reappears and ventures in to find it, it will have the power to wake the dead who are resting in the Catacombs."

He took a deep breath and rolled the glowing stone in his hands.

"Then I say we destroy it!" a worried voice rang out from somewhere in the crowd. A series of grumblings followed in agreement.

But Jacques shook his head. "This is a very powerful object. Destroying it would also lead to a catastrophic event for the city of Paris."

That quieted the crowd quickly.

"What if we hid it?" another voice suggested.

Now Jacques nodded slowly. "That is my thinking as well. But we must do more than hide the Rose de France. It must also be guarded."

"Won't that draw attention to its location?" someone asked.

"That, or help hide it in plain sight," Jacques said.

Another series of grumblings passed through the crowd of families, this time a little less worried.

After much more discussion, they were all in agreement. The Rose de France would be given to the Louvre, one of the world's most highly regarded museums for art and artifacts. Since it was located in the heart of Paris, the families could keep their eyes on the Rose de France while it remained protected alongside the thousands of other items of interest displayed within the museum.

A perfect choice for safely hiding something in plain sight.

Jacques Guillaume thanked the families for their attendance in the Catacombs, finally dismissing them to navigate back through the various tunnel systems they had taken to get there.

As they filed out, Jacques made his way to one young girl who'd been at the back of the gathering with her family. "Claudine," he said under his breath so the last of the people leaving wouldn't hear him.

As she turned to face him, she swept her long, dark hair and her new red scarf behind her shoulders, revealing a thin necklace lying against her chest. At the end of the chain dangled a small stone with matching white and purple streaks across its surface. Like the Rose de France, it glowed dimly in the dark room.

"Yes, Jacques?" Claudine asked, her eyes wide.

"You will continue to protect the key, won't you?" he asked her.

She nodded with the conviction of someone much older than herself. "Of course. And so will any family who comes after me. Just like you asked."

He smiled gently. "Good." Then he patted her on the back as his eyes swept up and around the chamber, taking in its dozens of grave markers. "I shudder to think what might occur should the wrong family heirs find their way here with both the key and the Rose de France in hand."

Jacques and Claudine were the last to leave the secret chamber. A rumbling boulder rolled into place, sealing the doorway behind them, once again leaving the space as silent as the bones that filled it.

CHAPTER 1
THE POSSIBILITIES OF PARIS

This wasn't how "normal" birthdays were supposed to go.

Then again, my dad and I were pretty far from normal when it came to just about everything we did together.

I was currently on my hands and knees in the dirt beside him, the famous explorer and archaeologist Russell James. Once again, he'd been hired to help excavate a new finding in a distant part of the world, and as his daughter, I, Harley James, had come along for the journey. My dog, Daisy, had come too, and she was currently digging her salt-and-pepper paws through a discarded mound of dirt behind us.

We'd arrived in France just two days ago, and although I was supposed to have my twelfth birthday off, this dig in the countryside turned out to be much bigger than Dad anticipated. He'd asked for my help with the excavation today in particular because a few members of the team were holed up in bed with a nasty cold.

Sure, it would have been nice to kick back for the day, but who was I to turn down an opportunity to get my hands dirty? Literally.

"Pass me that spade, would you, Harley?" he asked, wiping a

hand across his sweaty forehead and smudging it with dirt. "Whew! Warm today."

I sat back on my heels and pushed my blonde hair behind an ear carefully, so I wouldn't also get dirt where it didn't belong. I reached for the small tool in a pile on my left and also dug a bottle of water out of my purple backpack.

Now this isn't just any purple backpack. My mother gave it to me when I was little, before she passed away. It was covered in patches showing all the places around the world we'd been. I was eager to add one for France to my collection. Specifically for Paris. That is, if we ever got to go.

Though the French countryside was very nice, I was already itching to go to Paris and explore. The sprawling city just a few hours from where we were staying during the dig had endless things to see and do. I'd even read in the French guidebook my dad had given me that Paris had over a hundred museums for people to visit, the most impressive being the Louvre. It was jam-packed with thousands of art pieces and artifacts. While I could pass on the art, the artifacts practically called my name.

As a seasoned agent of S.M.A.L.L. (that's the Society of Mysterious Artifacts, Legends, and Lore), I had made it somewhat of a hobby to familiarize myself with ancient items whenever I got the chance.

You know, just in case there was an ancient, powerful object that might destroy the world if it got into the wrong hands.

S.M.A.L.L. had picked me to be an agent because I was great with cryptography and solving riddles and other puzzles. At least, I *think* that's why they chose me. As far as secret societies go, they might be the most secretive I'd ever heard of.

But that's the point of secret societies, right? That most people haven't heard of them?

Anyways, the problem with me wanting to go to Paris was that we had only been on this dig for two days. That meant there was no way my dad would be ready to leave anytime soon.

However—I had a plan. As Dad took a long swig from the water bottle, I eyed the other thing sitting inside my backpack that I'd hopefully be handing him soon: a permission slip for a summer program in Paris. I'd found the group online. It was a chaperoned event that bused kids into the city for a week to show them around and allow them to get a feel for the culture. I'd found the group online.

I'd already printed the permission slip out at our hotel, filled it all in, and just needed my dad's signature. But I was nervous to ask him about going. He pretty much *never* let me go anywhere without him because he was so overprotective.

I was twelve now, though. The thought of exploring a big city without my dad hovering a few steps behind me was exciting.

So today, on the dig, I planned to be on my best behavior. That way, tonight, back in our hotel room where he wouldn't be distracted, I'd ask if I could go on the trip. Y'know, as a sort of birthday present.

"I'll be right back, Harley. Gotta go check how the east-side unit is doing with their excavation," my dad said as he pushed himself up from the ground and walked away.

Daisy yipped at me from atop her pile of dirt, almost like she was asking me what was on my mind.

"Oh, nothing. Just big cities, bright lights, and baguettes," I told her with a pat on the head, accidentally smudging dirt across her white fur.

SEVERAL HOURS LATER, we wrapped up at the site for the day and headed back to the hotel.

Now we were relaxing in the living room of our little cottage suite. It wasn't the nicest or newest hotel we'd ever stayed in on one of our trips. The faded yellow wallpaper was peeling in a few corners. The wooden furniture creaked loudly if you so much as looked at it. The cushions and pillows had a bit of a musty smell. But the whole place had what Dad liked to call "old world charm" that made it comfortable.

Dad was currently sitting in an overstuffed armchair reading the latest edition of *Archaeology* magazine. His curly brown hair shook as he nodded his head, probably because he was agreeing with some kind of digging philosophy or expedition he was reading about. Though he'd cleaned most of the dirt from the day's dig off him, he was still wearing his red field scarf and blue shirt, which sprinkled a few flecks of dried muck onto the floor.

I sat across the room in a smaller chair, mustering up the courage to ask the question I'd been practicing all day.

"Um, Dad?"

"What's up, Cat-Cat?" he asked without looking up from his reading. Using my nickname meant he was in a good mood. That could work in my favor.

"Do you think we'll have time to go to Paris on this trip?"

"I dunno. It's a few hours away, and this dig has me pretty busy. I can't make any promises."

That's what I figured he'd say. "But it'd be a shame to pass up an opportunity to visit a city with so much history, wouldn't it?" I suggested.

"I suppose so, but these things happen sometimes," he said, flipping a page.

I decided to go for it. "Well, it doesn't have to happen that way!" I jumped up from my chair and pulled the permission slip from my pocket. "I found a group that chaperones kids for a week in Paris! They take us to see the sights, like the Eiffel Tower, museums, and even a botanical garden. It'd make for a pretty great birthday gift, don't you think?"

I dropped the form in his lap so he could read about it. He slowly put his magazine down, then looked back and forth between me and the permission slip. "Leave? Go to Paris? Without me?" he asked, his voice filled with confusion.

I nodded excitedly. "It looks really cool, Dad! And plenty safe. There's a chaperone who sets curfews and everything."

He took his time reading through all the trip details, his expression never changing. Maybe things weren't working in my favor after all.

"Hmmm," he finally said after what felt like forever. He turned the form over and over, looking for anything he might have missed.

I sighed. "I just thought that maybe—"

But he held up his hand. "Y'know, this might be good for you. Give you a chance to learn about an incredible city. Not to mention, start getting a feel for the importance of independence."

My jaw nearly dropped to the floor. "So...I can go?"

Dad smiled, pulled a pen from his shirt pocket, clicked it open, and signed on the dotted line. I was in a daze as he handed the form to me. But as I reached for it, he snatched it back. "Under one condition," he said, his smile fading. "No wandering off or getting into any trouble like you sometimes do."

I beamed and nodded excitedly again, and he finally handed the paper to me. "Deal!" I told him, practically skipping back to my room with Daisy on my heels.

I was going to Paris for educational purposes only. What kind of trouble could I possibly get into?

CHAPTER 2
BUBBLING WITH CURIOSITY

It was a lot harder to say goodbye to my dad than I thought it would be. Even though I was going to be just three hours away from him and only gone for a week.

"Learn lots, then come back and tell me all about it, okay?" he said as we waited for the group bus to Paris to arrive. "I want the full Harley report!"

We were standing in our hotel lobby, where a television was blaring the news. But it was all in French, and as I'd only learned a few words and phrases before our arrival, most of it was lost on me. So I wasn't paying it much attention, even though the news anchor did seem overly excited about something...

Instead, I nodded at my dad and swallowed a big lump in my throat. I was nervous, but I didn't want to admit it. I hiked my overstuffed backpack up higher on my shoulders and gripped Daisy's leash tightly in my fist. Thankfully, the chaperones had agreed to let me bring her along. Actually, it was my dad who had politely convinced them to make an exception to their rules. In the past,

Daisy had stuck by my side through thick and thin, so he felt better that she'd be with me.

"What's wrong, Cat-Cat? Aren't you excited?" my dad asked, squatting down to look me in the eyes.

I nodded again. "Uh-huh. Very," I told him. Really, I was. I was just having a hard time showing it at the moment.

But I started feeling better with a quick smile and a tight bear hug from my dad. I really *was* excited to be striking out on my own and exploring one of the most incredible cities in the world.

The bus finally pulled up to the curb outside the hotel entrance just as a few words on the TV caught my attention. Actually, it was two specific words the anchor had said: "Le Louvre."

I glanced up to see the anchor looking wide-eyed as he reported something about the famous museum. But what?

"Dad, what are they saying?" I asked, pointing to the flat screen on the wall.

"Hm? Oh, well, you know my French isn't great..." He squinted up at the TV. "But if I didn't know any better, I'd say something was stolen from the museum. Some kind of artifact?" Then he mumbled something about a lack of security but was too distracted by the arrival of the bus outside to translate anything else.

After another fierce hug, I climbed onto the bus. There were a bunch of kids my age, settling into their seats with small backpacks and big smiles. I found a window seat for Daisy and I, anxious to watch as the hills of France rolled by.

Our tour guide, Madame DeFleur stood at the front of the bus and gave some brief history as we made our way closer to Paris.

My head should have been filled with all the excitement that awaited me in Paris. But I couldn't help but wonder how someone had managed to get away with stealing something from one of the most secure museums in the world.

And let's just say I have a history with stolen artifacts.

By the time the bus wound its way into the sprawling city of Paris, all thoughts of stolen artifacts had fallen from my mind.

There was so much to see outside the window that I had a hard time keeping up! Old stone buildings containing homes, shops, and restaurants, funny little cars zipping by, and more historical statues and monuments than I could count. I even managed to glimpse the Eiffel Tower off in the distance as we rounded a corner to our destination.

Our first stop was the Jardin des Plantes, one of France's most famous botanical gardens. We all piled out of the bus, Daisy by my side, and were given time to stretch our legs in the main courtyard after the long ride. There were walls of green and incredible splashes of color all around me in the form of some of the most beautiful flowers I had ever seen.

I immediately slipped my phone from my pocket to snap some photos. "Dad said he wanted the full report," I reminded Daisy. Then I found myself wondering if this place had any daisies. Posing her in front of them would make for a *great* picture...

But my phone pinged and vibrated in my hand, distracting me. It was a text from an unknown number. All it read was: "*Go to the fountain.*"

Huh? What fountain?

I glanced around, and sure enough, there was a giant, round fountain across the courtyard. It was made of some kind of green stone and had statues of men and women all the way around it. Even from this distance, I could see that it was old, which meant I was already intrigued. This mysterious text only added to my curiosity.

I swung my purple backpack over my shoulders. I kept all the necessities inside; a cell phone, laptop, colored pencils, a leather notebook, gum, and a headlamp—just in case.

I snuck away from the chaperone, who was still busy gathering her belongings from the bus. But by the time I crossed the courtyard to the fountain, whoever was on the other end of that text hadn't shown.

I stood there all alone, the only sound the bubbling water filling the fountain at my feet. Why would someone text me instructions that led to nothing in particular?

They wouldn't. There must be more to find.

I pocketed my phone and searched the fountain high and low. But it was Daisy who found the tiny piece of parchment curled tightly up under the lip of the fountain. "Good girl!" I told her as she barked and licked my face.

I unraveled the paper and was excited to find a riddle written on it. I loved riddles.

I have a head and a tail
but I do not have a body.
I sometimes wish for one
while others wish on me.
What am I?

It was too easy. I'd heard this riddle before. Or at least some variation of it.

"A coin," I said out loud. Just in case whoever sent the text might have been hiding in the bushes somewhere, listening.

But nothing happened. This part of the courtyard was still and empty, with only the continued gurgling water of the fountain breaking the silence.

The fountain...

I glanced down into the pool of water and saw a single silver coin sitting at its bottom. It was the only coin I could see from this angle. Could that mean something?

Only one way to find out.

I dipped my hand into the cold water up to my elbow and retrieved the coin. It was bigger than it had looked, and underwater, I hadn't been able to see what was on the coin's face. It was a very familiar symbol showing an owl with a crescent moon crown.

None other than someone from S.M.A.L.L. had texted my phone, left the riddle, and placed the coin for me to find. Why was I not surprised?

I flipped the coin over to find an engraved image of the Eiffel Tower. It could have been just a souvenir from a gift shop. But I knew better.

Paris was turning even more exciting than I hoped it would be.

CHAPTER 3
TOWER OF TROUBLE?

I barely slept that night in the tiny room of the hotel where the group was staying near the center of Paris. I was tossing, turning, and thinking the day over.

What could S.M.A.L.L. possibly need me for this time around? Not that I wasn't willing to help them. It was an honor to be a member of the secret society. I'd felt that way ever since the day they'd invited me to join them during my and dad's visit to Tikal, Guatemala. Their mission to protect the world from dangerous ancient artifacts wasn't only admirable—it was necessary. I'd learned that much after having had several run-ins with various dastardly people trying to use dangerous artifacts to stir up trouble.

Thankfully, I'd been able to team up with other S.M.A.L.L. agents for these missions. Together, we'd always managed to retrieve the artifact in question and keep the world at peace.

S.M.A.L.L.'s motto was simple: *Preserve. Protect. Persevere.* I often repeated it to myself when I was in a sticky situation.

But if I was being honest, I was kind of looking forward to taking a break from it all. This was my first time away from my dad and my first chance to exercise my independence in a city with endless things to explore. Who knew when I'd be back here again?

By the time morning rolled around, I'd decided to meet this mysterious person at the Eiffel Tower. Duty was calling, and my curiosity had also gotten the better of me.

After changing out of my pajamas, I pulled my laptop out of my backpack to look up any helpful information on the Eiffel Tower. The tower itself was unveiled at the Paris World Exposition in March 1889. Ten years later, it was nearly torn down, but the Parisians realized they could use it as a radio tower. I dug a little deeper; there was actually a military bunker underneath. Now that was interesting.

The tower happened to be only a few blocks away from my hotel. Again, I shouldn't be surprised that S.M.A.L.L. likely knew my whereabouts.

Luckily, this mystery person sent a text that they wanted to meet at eight o'clock that morning. That would give me plenty of time to slip out, meet up, and then be back before my group was ready to leave for a visit to the Palace of Versailles at nine.

I grabbed my backpack and Daisy's leash, and off we went to find out what was going on.

But when Daisy and I got there, I thought maybe I'd made a mistake. We walked around the Eiffel Tower, but there was nothing but a bunch of tourists and a few gift shops.

"Well, that's weird," I said more to myself than to anyone around me.

What was I supposed to do now?

That's when my phone buzzed. It was another text from the same unknown number. This time it said: *"This is no mistake."* Then I got another text right after that. It was just a giant green arrow pointing me straight ahead. I looked up and saw a small pond with a stone walkway around it.

Before I could question it, Daisy startled me with a few loud barks and took off. Her leash slipped right out of my hand. "Daisy, no! Come back!" I yelled after her.

But she had already disappeared.

I couldn't just let her run free around the Eiffel Tower, so I picked up my pace and followed in the general direction she had gone. I found Daisy in the middle of the open space, sniffing around. Maybe she'd gotten an old whiff of croissants or something.

My stomach growled at the thought.

But there was nothing in this place. Just like I'd suspected from the street. "Come on, Daisy, let's get out of here," I told her as I bent to pick up her leash.

Maybe I could contact Deacon from S.M.A.L.L. back at my hotel room and find out what I was missing.

Daisy seemed to be onto something, though. She was sniffing a part of the stone courtyard off to the side I hadn't noticed before. The stones on the ground were loose. And they were arranged in a unique way, almost like a puzzle.

I glanced around me. Tourists and guides were everywhere, but no one seemed to notice the little courtyard I had found. The landscaping around the area seemed to be giving us some privacy. I knelt down on the ground to touch the stones.

"What'd you find, girl?"

The puzzle was made of a series of small tiles, all in a jumbled order that didn't add up to anything I could recognize. There were fifteen pieces in all and one empty space in the middle of them.

"I know what this is," I said as I shifted the pieces around. One by one, I had to slide them into just the right place to make an image come together. But this was harder than the kind of puzzle you find in a box because you don't know what image you're trying to make all the pieces add up to.

It took a while, but after nearly ten minutes of sliding all the little tiles around, a picture finally formed beneath my fingertips. And I recognized it from the guidebook my dad had given me.

It was the French symbol of peace. It was similar to a normal four-pronged peace sign but was slightly altered to include the Eiffel Tower.

Before I could wonder why this symbol would be here of all places, a low rumbling started from somewhere beneath my feet. Daisy matched it with her own quiet growl, then stood up from the ground.

That's where I found the source of the rumbling. A thick concrete panel in the ground was sliding away to reveal a gaping hole below. And there was a sloping ramp leading away from the entrance. Completing the puzzle must have been the key to unlocking it.

"Hello?" I called down into the dark. But there was no answer. I looked around—no one was paying us any attention. "Well, here goes nothing," I told Daisy as I stepped onto the ramp and began my descent. She followed after me cautiously.

The stiff air around me instantly got colder. As I walked deeper and deeper in, getting further and further away from the light of the entryway, it was so dark that I couldn't even see my hand in front of my face.

I turned on my phone flashlight and lifted it out in front of me to illuminate the tunnel. Then I took a deep breath and remembered all the great work I'd done with S.M.A.L.L. up until this point. *Preserve. Protect. Persevere.* I took a few more steps.

Then I nearly screamed as the light's beam caught the bright green eyes of someone staring right back at me.

CHAPTER 4
BENEATH THE SURFACE

"Please do not be alarmed, Harley James," a soft voice said. My pulse was pounding so hard in my ears that I almost didn't hear it.

The light from my phone was bouncing up and down in my trembling hands. It revealed a young girl, probably only a few years older than me, with vibrant green eyes and long, kettle-black hair. She wore a black-and-white-striped shirt and a red beret like she had just walked off a French postcard.

Her expression was serious but not scary. I took a deep breath.

The light also caught the glimmer of a medallion hanging from her neck. It matched the same medallion I owned, with the same symbol that had been on the coin from the fountain.

"You're an agent of S.M.A.L.L.?" I finally managed to squeak out.

The girl nodded, then clicked on a flashlight. It illuminated the narrow tunnel, bringing me an instant sense of relief. But only for a moment because this passageway was really, really tiny. I hoped I wouldn't start feeling claustrophobic.

"My name is Veronica Rousseau. Now follow me," the girl said with a heavy French accent. Before I could stick out my hand for a shake, Veronica was whirling around to continue quickly down the sloping path.

"Nice to meet you," I murmured under my breath, deciding not to complain about being scared half to death.

We walked in single file silently for a few minutes, the tunnel still sloping down for a while before finally evening out. But a glance ahead into the darkness didn't reveal where the end of this thing was. How far under the city could we possibly be now? I wanted to ask Veronica (along with about a million other questions), but the clacking of our shoes and Daisy's nails against the stone floor felt like they were taking up all the room for conversation down here.

"Why do you have this dog?" Veronica finally broke the silence. But she didn't turn around or even slow down.

"Who, Daisy?"

She nodded curtly.

I wasn't sure how I felt about this girl. It almost seemed like I was bothering her or something. Even though she was clearly the one who was texting my phone and leaving me riddles and puzzles to solve.

"Daisy goes everywhere with me. She's my travel buddy and has even been a bit of a good luck charm when it comes to solving riddles or codes. In fact, I don't think I've ever solved one on a S.M.A.L.L. mission without her around," I said with a proud chuckle.

Veronica gave a short laugh, but I wasn't sure if she was laughing with me or at me. This whole meeting felt very rushed and strange.

Okay, it was time to get some answers. I stopped walking. So did Daisy.

It took a few steps before Veronica realized that I was no longer right behind her. "Harley, what is wrong? We must keep moving," she said as she walked back toward me.

"I just need you to answer some questions for me. It'd be nice to know what's going on," I told her.

Just outside the glowing circle of her flashlight, I barely made out Veronica rolling her eyes. "No one has briefed you?" she asked.

"Briefed me? Uhhh, no. Sorry."

She sighed. "No, I am sorry. I do not mean to be so short with you. I did not realize no one had told you about the disaster we face."

My eyebrows rose in surprised shock all on their own. Disaster? Well, that didn't sound good. I definitely didn't feel equipped to face a disaster. "What do you mean?" I asked her.

She circled the beam of her flashlight along the walls around us. "Can you guess where we are right now?" she asked.

I shrugged. "Somewhere underneath the city, I would think."

"*Oui*." She nodded, speaking in French. *Oui* means "yes" and was about the only French word I knew. Veronica switched to English. "But it is more specific than that. We are currently standing in one of the tunnels that is part of the Catacombs of Paris."

I'd heard of the Catacombs before and even read a few things about it in my guidebook. But after a couple paragraphs, I'd felt a little too creeped out to keep reading. "Aren't the Catacombs filled with...um...human bones?" I asked with a quick glance around. Thankfully, I didn't see any bones sticking out of the stone walls.

"*Oui*, the bones of over six million people. The Catacombs consist of hundreds of miles of tunnels connecting to chambers filled with a variety of items. Mostly bones, but also important artifacts in some cases."

This was starting to get interesting. Maybe I should have put the Catacombs on my list of must-visit places in Paris after all.

"One of the deepest and most difficult chambers to find in the

Catacombs was once home to a very important artifact," Veronica continued. "One that has now gone missing from the Louvre."

That sounded familiar. "Hey, I think I saw something about that on the news yesterday," I realized. "What was it?"

"It is called the Rose de France," Veronica explained. "And if whoever stole it from the museum brings it back to that specific chamber, it has the power to make all the bones resting in the Catacombs come back to life."

A shiver ran down my spine. "And what happens when the bones come alive?" I asked reluctantly.

Veronica shook her head. "That all depends on what the person who brought them to life *wants* them to do. But I'm afraid it wouldn't be anything good."

I agreed with her there. Why would someone want millions of creepy old bones to come to life if not to use them for some terrifying purpose? And once the bones were alive…well, could you even lay something to rest that was already dead? Could the bones ever be stopped?

"Whoever has the Rose de France commands the bones," Veronica explained. "But before they can do that, they will also need a specific key to get into the chamber where the ritual must be performed in the first place. A key that I know for a fact this person does not have."

"How do you know?" I asked her.

"Because I have it," Veronica stated.

She shined her flashlight on her necklace, where her S.M.A.L.L. medallion was hanging. But when she moved it aside, hanging just behind it was a perfectly round amethyst gem.

"This has been passed down in my family for generations," she told me. "And now, I need your help making sure it remains in my hands."

CHAPTER 5
GETTING UP TO SPEED

I looked at the little stone with curiosity. "It's pretty, but how is that a key? It's just a rock."

Veronica frowned at me. "This *rock* is a piece of the Rose de France itself. Without it, the chamber cannot be opened, and the ritual cannot be performed."

"What ritual?" I asked.

"Well, the legend says that a small drop of blood from one of the ancient bloodlines must be placed in a small bowl inside a secret chamber deep in the catacombs. The Rose de France must then be placed on top. Once the blood touches the stone, the ritual is complete."

My eyes went wide. *Blood? A secret chamber?* This definitely fell into the legends and lore category.

"But in order for the ritual to work, they must have both the key and the Rose de France." She swallowed. "And I worry that whoever was able to figure out how to get past security at the Louvre will be able to find a way to get this key from my family."

Now it was all coming together. If you had told me two years ago that a small stone could bring millions of dead bones to life, I wouldn't have believed it. But after what happened with my last three missions for S.M.A.L.L., I knew to take her seriously.

"So that's why S.M.A.L.L. needs our help. We must find whoever stole the Rose de France and get it back. If they make it to the secret chamber with the stone, it's bad news for everyone."

My brow furrowed. "Aren't the police looking into the Louvre robbery? Won't they be able to find the stone?"

Veronica let out a sigh and rolled her eyes. "The police have been useless. They have no leads, and have made no progress. It's up to us."

"What about your parents? Can they help us?"

Veronica shook her head. "They are in the United States, on holiday. There is no way they can make it back here in time to help us."

I felt the weight of the mission settling onto my shoulders.

"Okay, I'm in," I said after a deep breath.

Veronica tapped my shoulder and looked me in the eyes. "This is our most important mission yet, Harley."

Now that I was all caught up, she turned and started walking down the tunnel again. I had to speed walk to keep up with her.

Every few steps, we were hit with a cold burst of air coming from the opening of yet another tunnel leading away from ours... and another...and another, until I lost count of how many we passed. I swear I even spotted a giant gray rat scurrying down one of them, and Daisy did too. If I hadn't been gripping her leash, she would have gone chasing off into the darkness after it.

As we kept descending, the tunnel around us started feeling oddly damp. The old stones lining the walls were slick with what I hoped was just water trickling in from somewhere above us. I had to walk carefully to make sure I didn't slip.

The path we walked was worn, like lots of feet had passed this way at some point. And yet, it was so still both in front of and behind us that I wondered how much time had passed since anyone had been in this particular tunnel at all.

"Raising the dead in the Catacombs would have terrible consequences. We can't let it happen," Veronica stressed again, pulling me from my thoughts.

"So what can we do? Just stay hidden down here forever?" I asked.

"Now that the Rose de France has been stolen, we must perform a ritual of our own. One that will keep the bones at rest permanently."

"Well, how do we do that?"

"First, we must find our way to the hidden chamber and access it before they do."

My trip to Paris was suddenly starting to turn out much different than I had hoped for. This mission sounded dangerous. Hundreds of miles of chambers was a huge maze to navigate. What if we got lost? What if the key didn't work? Or what if we came face to face with whoever had stolen the Rose de France? I had no idea who we were up against or where things could really lead.

That's when it dawned on me that we'd been walking for an awfully long time.

"Hey, Veronica, where are we going?" I asked. "We're not trying to find the chamber now, are we?"

Just then, to my relief, the tunnel began to slope upward under our feet. As we made our way up, I even started hearing some faint, muffled noise from the city streets above us.

"No, we aren't prepared to find the chamber yet," Veronica said. "According to the legend, there is a secret map that will lead us through the maze to a very secret entrance of the room we are looking for."

Thank goodness, I thought. There was a map. That would at least make things a little easier. "So, where is this map?" I asked.

We had come to a fork in the tunnel. The left side led back down into a darkness I hoped we weren't about to head into. The right side continued sloping upward.

"It is somewhere in the building above us," Veronica said. "And I am definitely going to need your help retrieving it." She motioned for me to follow her up the right tunnel (whew!), where we came to a small metal grate just above our heads. Through its open slats, I could see the blue sky above.

"Where are we?" I asked.

"Just outside the Hôtel national des Invalides," Veronica said as she clicked off her flashlight and put it in her pocket. Then she reached into a different pocket for a screwdriver and started unscrewing the grate. "I led us here through a shallow tunnel of the Catacombs to make sure we were not followed."

That made sense to me. "So the map is inside a hotel?" I asked.

"Sort of," was all she replied. With a clang, she popped the grate open and hauled herself out. Then she reached a hand back down to help me. Instead, I lifted Daisy up and handed her out to Veronica. She seemed hesitant at first, but with a friendly lick of her hand, Daisy buttered her up, and Veronica grasped her gently.

I pulled myself up and through the grate next, blinded by the sudden brightness of the morning after being down in the dingy dark for so long. The fresh air was a welcome relief.

My eyes adjusted to see an enormous building right behind us. It wasn't like any hotel I'd ever seen before. The old stone building sprawled for several blocks, with a big, domed tower in the middle of it. I suspected it wasn't actually a hotel at all.

"What is this place?" I asked.

Veronica finished screwing the grate back into the sidewalk, then wiped her hands clean. "Among other things, this is the home of the Musée des Plans-Reliefs."

"In English?" I asked softly.

"The Museum of Relief Maps," she explained. "And *that* is where the map we're looking for is kept."

Oh no. I'd been in a situation like this before. I knew what was coming next.

"We're going to go and steal the map, aren't we?" I asked Veronica.

She smirked. "More like borrow it. If we can get past all the puzzles and riddles guarding it, that is."

Puzzles and riddles? Now she was speaking my language.

CHAPTER 6
AN UNEXPECTED VISITOR

"I did some researching online," Veronica told me as we started down the sidewalk. She ignored the surprised stares of several tourists who had just watched two girls and a dog emerge from beneath the ground.

"I discovered a forum discussing the map of the Catacombs we are looking for. The theory is that the museum owner is hiding it away in the most secure room of his collection," Veronica explained.

"Wait, it's just a theory?" I tucked an unruly strand of blonde hair behind my ear. "As in, we're not even one hundred percent sure it's in there?"

She nodded. "Unfortunately, yes. But I have a good feeling about it. None of my research pointed to any other location as a possible option."

She seemed confident enough.

The area outside the Hôtel national des Invalides was busy. Veronica explained that this building was a center for tourism, with a variety of museums, shops, and other venues to explore.

But the Musée des Plans-Reliefs was the particular place we aimed to "explore" that morning.

According to Veronica, it was a peculiar museum that displayed a variety of maps from all around France in some interesting ways. And the curator of the museum was also peculiar in that he didn't let just anyone access the part of the museum that housed the most prized maps from his collection. I was excited to see what, exactly, she meant by that.

But my excitement was cut short when my cell phone started ringing. It was my dad. "Sorry, just a sec. He's probably just checking in on me," I told Veronica as I answered the call. "Hey, Dad, what's up?"

"There you are!" he said. "I've been trying to call you for the last twenty minutes, but it wouldn't go through."

That was probably thanks to being underground. "Oh, sorry. I was...uhhh, on a tour of the city," I told him. It wasn't exactly a lie.

"Wow, early tour time," he said.

I hadn't thought about that. It *was* still early. And I would have to head back to my hotel soon so the group and chaperone wouldn't think I'd gone missing. I decided I'd return just as soon as we took a look inside the Musée des Plans-Reliefs.

"Yeah, they managed to squeeze us in before anyone else," I sort of fibbed.

"Well, think you'll have some time to squeeze me into your day?" he asked, a sly note in his voice.

I narrowed my eyes, even though he couldn't see me doing it through the phone. "What's that supposed to mean?" I asked him.

"I'm in Paris! Surprise!" he said.

My heart skipped a beat. "Really? What are you doing in Paris?" I asked.

"That cold going around on the dig crew got worse. So we decided to postpone work for a few days while everyone recovered.

Seeing as I'm feeling fine, I thought I'd meet up with you in the city and tag along on your sightseeing!"

Dad was really excited. I could hear it in his voice. But I suddenly had very mixed feelings about everything. As much as I already missed him, he'd said so himself: This trip was a great opportunity to learn about being independent. And that's exactly what I'd intended to do. Now he was here? And wanting to tag along on everything? Didn't that kind of defeat the purpose of me taking this trip on my own?

Don't get me wrong, I loved spending time with my dad. But I had so much I wanted to do in Paris. And now a pretty serious S.M.A.L.L. mission on top of everything!

"So, where should I meet you?" he asked on the other end of the line, that pure excitement in his voice growing.

I didn't have the heart to turn him away.

"Back at our hotel. We're regrouping there at nine," I said.

"Great, I'm only a few blocks away. See you soon, Harley!" And he hung up.

I pocketed my phone and avoided looking down at Daisy. She was staring at me with her big, brown, questioning eyes like she knew I hadn't been entirely truthful with my dad.

"What was that about?" Veronica asked.

"My dad is in town, and I have to go meet up with him. Just give me a couple of hours." I tucked my thumbs into my backpack. "I'm so sorry, can we visit the museum later? I'll text you. We'll find the map then, I promise."

Veronica frowned and fumbled with her red beret. "Later? I suppose it can wait, though I do not like the idea of delaying. Especially when we don't know where this person who has the Rose de France is or what they are up to." She shook her head as she looked up at the building we would no longer be entering. "But go if you must."

I felt terrible. All the trust we had quickly built in that tunnel seemed to be slipping away. But I didn't have any choice. I couldn't explain to my dad where I was or what I was about to do. I was supposed to be staying out of trouble, after all.

"Thanks, Veronica. I promise you'll hear from me soon," was all I could think to say. And I hoped it was a promise I could keep.

IT WAS NEARLY four in the afternoon before I could safely text Veronica that I was finally ready to meet back up with her.

Daisy and I had arrived back at the hotel that morning just in time to watch my dad pull up in a cab out front. At nearly the same time, the chaperone from the trip came into the lobby, leading the other kids behind her.

We'd all spent the morning touring the Palace of Versailles and the afternoon exploring various eateries around the city offering French delicacies. The chaperone seemed thankful to have my dad around as another pair of eyes. I had to admit, it was really fun and interesting to have him read facts from my guidebook to the whole group. He had a lot more insights into Parisian history than I'd realized.

The group had parted ways in the hotel lobby to freshen up for that evening's activity: a bus tour to see the city lit up at night. My plan was to slip out, go to the Musée des Plans-Reliefs with Veronica, and be back before we left for the tour.

And working to my advantage, Dad yawned widely and stretched his arms wide as he said, "I think I'll turn in early. Let you take this tour solo. Daisy can come with me for the evening too."

Whew! I wasn't sure dogs were allowed inside the Hôtel national des Invalides. And she definitely wouldn't be allowed in the Musée des Plans-Reliefs.

That was when I texted Veronica and told her to meet me there in thirty minutes.

"Sounds good, Dad. Thanks for today. It was actually fun," I said.

He stopped mid-stretch and stared at me. "*Actually* fun? Were you worried it wouldn't be?" he asked.

Oops. A slip of the tongue.

"No, I mean—not worried—I just—I didn't mean…" I stammered around for an explanation.

But Dad just laughed and put an arm around my shoulders. "It's all right, Harley. You don't have to explain. I get it."

"You do?"

"Well, sure," he said as he and Daisy headed for the front door. "You didn't want the other kids getting jealous because they don't get to have a parent on this trip."

Oh. He didn't really get it after all.

But I just mustered up a smile for him. "Right again, Dad."

He smiled back. "See you tomorrow," he said, then headed out onto the sidewalk and down the block to his own hotel.

I gave it a minute before I headed out right behind him.

CHAPTER 7
THE KEY TO THE PLAN

Veronica was crawling up through the same grate in the ground we had gone through earlier that morning just as I rounded the corner and came to the front of the Hôtel national des Invalides. With the hot summer day cooling off as evening approached, it seemed like there were even *more* tourists out and about than before.

I offered Veronica a hand and pulled her up onto the sidewalk from the Catacombs tunnel.

"And how was your day of playing tourist?" she asked as she put the grate back in place. I couldn't tell if she was being sarcastic or not.

"It was fine. I'm sorry I couldn't get away sooner. My dad can be...persistent," I tried to explain.

But she was already heading for the building, once again leaving me speed walking to try and keep up. She had a red scarf tied around her neck, which made her look very chic.

"I like your scarf," I said, trying to warm her up. She touched it lightly.

"Thank you, it was my Grandmother Claudine's," she replied.

Truthfully, I felt a little out of place here in Paris with my khaki shorts and white T-shirt. Everyone seemed so fashionable here.

Maybe I could convince Dad to take me shopping once the mission was over.

We entered the Hôtel national des Invalides. The inside was a big, open space made of impressive marble and stone. It was much quieter here than outside, as most tourists were leaving for the day. Maybe that would make sneaking out with a "borrowed" map a little easier.

We crossed the massive hall and headed down toward a sign that indicated the Musée des Plans-Reliefs. But when we got there, we spotted another, smaller sign hanging across the door that read "*Fermé.*"

"Oh no," Veronica said sharply.

"What is it? What's wrong?" I asked.

"That sign says the museum is closed."

"Oh no," I repeated back to her. We had come back too late. And it was all my fault.

Veronica said a few words in French under her breath that I couldn't understand. Which was probably a good thing. Then she switched back to English. "Now what are we supposed to do?" she asked, glancing up and down the long hall in desperation.

I followed her gaze to see a security guard sitting in a chair at the end of the hall. I also saw something that could very well solve our problem. "I have an idea," I told Veronica as I pointed to a small black box fitted to the museum door. It had a narrow slit in the top, with a glowing red light next to it. "This is the door's lock. It takes a key card to open," I said.

"Yes, but we do not have the key card."

"Not yet." I glanced back at the security guard and nodded in his direction. He had a variety of items dangling from his belt, including a walkie-talkie and a large flashlight. But next to those, on a retractable chain, was a slim black key card.

Veronica suddenly understood exactly what I was thinking. "You cannot be serious! He will not just hand it over and let us into a closed museum," she said with disbelief.

"You're right; he wouldn't. But I don't think that's going to be a problem," I said as I set off down the hall, moving as quickly as I could while tiptoeing. As we approached the guard, I pressed a finger to my lips. Veronica followed my lead. Only when we got closer did she notice the same thing I had from back down the hall: that the security guard's head was dropped to one side, almost touching his shoulder. And his eyes were closed.

It wasn't until we were right next to him that we both heard the unmistakable heavy breathing of snoring. "He's fast asleep!" I whispered. Some security team this was!

As Veronica stood watch to make sure no other security guards or interfering tourists were about to come around the corner, I crept up behind him and slowly reached for his key card. My shaking hand brushed up against the chain, which clanged loudly against the metal leg of the chair.

We both froze. The guard grunted loudly and rubbed his nose, shifting his head to his other shoulder. But his eyes didn't open. And after another few seconds, he went right back to snoring.

That was close.

I unclipped the card from the chain, and we both scurried back down the hall to the museum door. We had to move fast if we wanted to return the card before the guard woke up and realized it was missing.

I inserted the key into the top of the lock, and the little red light flashed from red to green.

"It worked! Excellent thinking, Harley!" Veronica said excitedly, patting me on the back.

Seemed like I had redeemed myself.

With a last glance around to see that the coast was clear, we wrenched open the door and snuck into the closed Musée des Plans-Reliefs.

CHAPTER 8
MUSÉE DES PLANS-RELIEFS

I had never walked into a room as dark as this one. The only pitch-black that rivaled it had been the darkness of the Catacombs tunnel where I had met Veronica that morning. And just as I had down there, I waved my hands in front of my face to test my eyes.

But I couldn't see a thing. They might as well have been closed. "Flashlight?" I whispered to Veronica. A second later, she clicked it on and swept the beam of light around the room.

The Musée des Plans-Reliefs was not at all what I expected it to be. The space was filled to the brim with 3D renderings of scale models that detailed the history of France's military. There were sprawling tables showing displays of the entire country at different points in time, while other areas had model castles and forts reaching nearly to the ceiling.

I could only hope the map we were looking for was much smaller and flatter. Otherwise, how else would we get it out of here unnoticed?

"Follow me," Veronica whispered, even though it was clear there was no one else in this place. But you can never be too careful.

She made her way across the main area and to the back of the room. "The Catacombs map is kept in his private collection," she reminded me. "The owner only lets certain visitors into that room."

"How does he choose which visitors can go in?" I asked.

"He doesn't. Only the ones who can figure out his puzzles make it all the way through."

We were now standing in front of a large metal door that looked like a bank vault. There was another key card lock next to the door like the one outside, so for good measure, Veronica tried swiping the security guard's card. But it was no use. The little light stayed red.

"Okay, Harley James, this is where you come in," Veronica said. She pointed the flashlight beam at an iPad secured to the wall next to the door. Its screen was illuminated with a list of language options. I pressed "English," and up came two items that I instantly recognized. The first was a cipher. The second was a riddle.

I took a deep breath and reached for the screen again.

"Wait a second," Veronica suddenly said, spooking me. Had she heard something? Was someone coming? "I think this iPad is connected to the security system," she told me, pointing her flashlight up the wall and to the ceiling.

"What does that mean?" I asked her, my palms now getting sweaty with worry.

"It means that if you fail the puzzle, we are going to have some company. Some very angry company."

I pulled my hands back, thinking our situation over.

Is this really the right thing to do?

I had promised my dad I'd stay out of trouble. Even though he was now here in Paris with me, that promise shouldn't change. And potentially setting off an alarm inside a closed museum would certainly change it.

Still...this was important. Important enough that S.M.A.L.L. had recruited Veronica and me to help. And Veronica seemed to know a lot. She was the heir to the keepers of the key, after all. That had to make her like, one of the most important agents of the Society. I could trust her knowledge, right?

"And you're sure the map is somewhere in here?" I asked her again, just to double-check.

For the first time since I'd met her, Veronica hesitated. "I am not sure of anything. This is only a guess. At this point, you know as much as I do about this mission."

Well, now, *that* made sweat bead on my forehead as well as my hands.

"I will admit that S.M.A.L.L. told me they have very little information about where this mission might lead," she went on. "They asked me to start investigating only a few days ago. And when I heard you would be in town, I knew I could use your help." She smiled at me, her green eyes full of reassurance. "I know you can do it, Harley. I believe in you."

I took another deep breath. And another. The deep breaths were helping. I was glad Veronica believed in me...but did I believe in myself?

I could feel the heat rising under my arms and the sweat breaking out on my nose. If I got a piece of the puzzle wrong, not only would my trip to Paris be cut short, but millions of sets of bones underneath our feet right now could potentially be awakened to wreak destruction on humanity.

I didn't want something like that hanging over my head. So I had no choice. I had to at least try.

"The first thing we need to figure out is the cipher code," I said as I pushed some stray blonde hairs out of my eyes. I tapped that part of the screen to illuminate it. "I think what we are looking at is a Caesar Box."

"What's that?"

"It was a kind of code that Augustus Caesar invented in order to send secret messages to people. To the untrained eye, it looks like nothing more than a jumble of gobbledygook."

Veronica gave a nervous laugh. "Gobbledygook, right."

We both stared the letters:

G T Y O R J O T E O U I A B G T

"But to me, it looked like a possibility. I've come up against several Caesar Box codes in a handful of the cryptography competitions I've entered over the years….so here goes nothing."

Veronica watched me as I pulled out my notebook and began to jot down the letters. First, I divided the code into groups of four letters on the screen, one by one, arranging each group in horizontal lines:

G T Y O

R J O T

E O U I

A B G T

Next, I knew I needed to read each line, not left to right like you would do with normal writing, but vertically from top to bottom instead. That being the case, the Caesar Box read:

GREAT JOB YOU GOT IT

"I think this is it!"

My hands still trembling, I typed out the words and hit the Enter key. I squeezed my eyes shut and held my breath, waiting for a shrieking alarm to go off.

But it didn't. The museum stayed perfectly quiet...until a hissing sound started from somewhere.

"Harley, look!" Veronica said, shaking my shoulder.

I opened my eyes to see the vault release and open. But just a crack. It was barely enough to get an arm through, let alone our whole bodies. And no matter how hard we tugged on it, we couldn't get the heavy door to open any further.

"Time for the next puzzle, I guess," I told Veronica, tapping the second piece open on the iPad screen.

This one was a flat-out riddle, which was both good and bad. All you had to do was answer the question it asked. But the hard part was getting that answer exactly right.

I read the words on the screen out loud:

The moment you utter my name, I disappear. What am I?

My heart sank. I'd never heard this one before. It was so short you'd think it'd be easy. But sometimes, the short riddles were the trickiest of all.

I turned to Veronica for help, but she was at a loss too.

The moment you utter my name, I disappear.

What could it possibly be?

My hands trembled as they hovered over the keyboard. I had no idea what the correct answer was. And it's not like I could take a guess. We had one shot at this.

"Think, Harley, think," I whispered to myself, my soft voice cutting through the quiet of the empty museum. It was so quiet in this place that it was almost distracting.

It was so quiet that it made me realize...

"That's it!" I nearly yelled, startling Veronica. She shushed me quickly. "Sorry," I whispered. "But I think I've got the answer."

The moment you utter my name, I disappear. What am I?

I quickly typed in a single word on the screen below the question:

SILENCE

I hit the Enter key, and we both held our breath.

CHAPTER 9
READ BETWEEN THE LINES

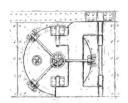

Before the vault had a chance to do anything, a loud noise reached us from outside the museum door.

"What was that?" Veronica whispered, her green eyes wide.

We both craned our ears to listen. It was someone shouting. Someone who sounded angry. But they were speaking in French, so I had no idea what they were saying.

"Mince!" Veronica hissed in French.

"What? What's wrong?"

"It is the security guard. He is awake from his nap. And he knows his key is missing," she translated for me.

Uh-oh.

"Well then, it's time to get inside this door and close it behind us," I told Veronica. "We need that map!"

But nothing was happening. No hissing of the vault door opening wider, no sounding alarm. Nothing. Just the echoing silence of the answer to the riddle.

"Is it broken?" Veronica asked. She pulled on the slightly ajar door for good measure, but it didn't budge.

"I don't know. Maybe I got the riddle wrong?" I said, though I was sure I hadn't. What else could the answer possibly be? I turned back to the iPad and stared it down. "Silence" had to be the right answer. So why was the door still stuck open so that no one could fit inside? It almost seemed like another puzzle to solve...

I tried peering through the cracked door and into the room beyond, but it was completely dark. And completely silent.

"Wait a minute," I said. "I think we need to be quiet."

"What do you mean?" Veronica asked.

"Well, 'silence' is the answer to the riddle. So maybe we need to be silent for the door to open all the way." I held a finger up to my lips for good measure, and Veronica nodded. We stayed completely silent and completely still.

But another angry shout echoed from outside, followed by an aggressive rattle of the museum's front door. How long would it be before that security guard got one of his buddies to use their key to open the door?

We didn't have time to find out.

But all we could do was stay quiet, wait, and hope that the guard would move away from the door long enough to give us the silence we needed.

I couldn't tell how much time passed with us just standing there, nervous sweat beading on our foreheads. But after what felt like an eternity, the shouting outside stopped. The Musée des Plans-Reliefs became utterly quiet.

And the vault door started to hiss open again.

"It worked!" Veronica mouthed silently, scared of making the door stop in its tracks.

But it opened all the way, and we slipped inside, being sure to clang the vault door closed behind us. Hopefully, it would buy us some time if those guards did make their way inside the museum.

"This is not what I expected," Veronica said from behind me. She swept her flashlight beam up and along the walls of the small yet high-ceilinged room, revealing three different balcony levels surrounding us. And on each level were rows and rows of shelved books.

Nothing that looked remotely map-like in sight.

"We're not going to find anything in this kind of dark," I said as I started sweeping my hands along the wall just inside the door. My fingers finally caught on a switch, and I flipped it up, washing the room in bright yellow light.

"Much better," Veronica said, clicking her flashlight off.

We might have had light now, but it still left us with a confusing room around us—where were all the maps?

"I thought you said the museum owner kept all his most private and rare maps in this room," I said to Veronica. "This is just a bunch of books."

Veronica frowned as she took in shelves upon shelves of brightly colored books. Most of them looked very old and worn. "Maybe the map is in a book?" she suggested.

I nodded. "It must be...but how do we know which one?"

The shelves suddenly seemed much taller and fuller than when we first entered the room. There had to be *hundreds* of books around us. No way would we have time to flip through them all to find the map to the secret Catacombs chamber.

"What else can you tell me about the owner of the museum?" I asked Veronica. "Why would he make people solve puzzles to access his private collection, only for them to find books instead of maps?"

Veronica took her phone out of her pocket and started scrolling through her Notes app. "It says here that he also owns a few private libraries around the city. So it would seem he is a collector of maps *and* books," she told me. "Does that mean anything?"

I walked into the center of the room and did a full turn, scanning the levels of books. "Maybe..." I said.

That's when my eye caught an arrangement of books on a shelf on the second level that looked odd. I mean, most of the books in here were odd, with cracked spines and flaking gold lettering in languages I couldn't read. But these particular books weren't so much odd as they were oddly *placed*.

"What does that look like to you?" I asked Veronica, pointing up to the second level.

She whirled around, her eyes wide. "Is that...an arrow?" she asked.

About twenty books with dark burgundy spines were laid out across three different shelves in a precise pattern that formed an arrow pointing up and to the right. If you weren't specifically looking for something different on the shelves, it'd be pretty easy to miss amongst all the other books.

"I think you're right," I said as I crossed the room, pushed a tall, rolling ladder out of one corner, and lined it up with the arrow bookshelves. Veronica was right behind me as I scampered up the wooden rungs, each step creaking beneath my shoes.

It was even harder to see the full arrow up close, but I had kept my eye on the last book in the pattern. The one that hopefully pointed to something useful.

Standing on the second level, I could see that the last burgundy book pointed to a thin, blue book on the shelf above it. It looked much newer than all the other books.

I slipped it carefully from its spot, but it got caught on something halfway out. So I put a little oomph behind it, and as I pulled, I heard a loud click from somewhere within the shelf.

Or more like behind the shelf.

Like the vault door, the bookshelf made a hissing noise as one side released from the wall and slowly swung open. Behind it was an even smaller room than the one we were in, with just enough space for the two of us to squeeze in.

But lining the walls of that room were about a dozen old maps.

"*Nous l'avons trouvé!*" Veronica shouted, jumping up and down. I gave her a curious look. "We found it," she said in a softer voice, translating for me.

Most of the old maps were behind protective glass cases or hung inside shimmering silver frames on the walls. But a small stand in one corner had a thick leather notebook sitting atop it, open to a page in the middle. And on that page was an intricately detailed map, decorated with tiny drawings of human skulls.

Except one of the drawings wasn't a skull. In the upper right corner of the map was a round circle with four squiggly lines drawn across it. I had no idea what that was about, but this had to be it! My heart was thumping with excitement.

But Veronica looked upset.

"What the matter? This is it, right? We found it?" I asked her.

"Yes, I do believe this is it," she said. "But I did not expect it to be inside a notebook. We cannot steal the entire thing. Look at it." She started flipping through it delicately. It was really old and worn. "This notebook is *filled* with tons of important French history. If we take this notebook and something goes wrong, we will lose much more than just a map."

I understood what she meant. History was important to preserve. And this notebook apparently had a lot of it. It didn't feel smart to take the whole thing.

"Why don't we just snap some photos then? With our phones?" I suggested instead. "That way, we don't have to 'borrow' anything."

Veronica nodded, clearly feeling at least a little relieved.

I retrieved my phone from my pocket and snapped a dozen

photos of the map from every angle I could think of. "That should do it," I said when I was done. "Now, let's get out of here."

We made our way out of the little map room, back down the ladder, out of the book vault, and back into the dark Musée des Plans-Reliefs, thankful to see that apparently, the guard had given up the search for his key card. On our way out, we casually dropped it on the floor outside the museum door for him to find.

Hopefully, our good luck would last long enough to finish this mission for good.

CHAPTER 10
LEGENDS OF THE CATACOMBS

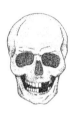

I watched Dad devour his second ham and cheese baguette sandwich that morning. I had barely taken a few bites out of my croissant with blackberry jam. Delicious as it was, I was too distracted by the previous evening's events to think much about my appetite.

We were sitting out on the balcony of Dad's tenth-floor hotel room, enjoying breakfast. The tour group had been given a free morning to explore the city independently, so naturally, Dad had suggested we have breakfast and plan the rest of our morning together.

I didn't mind much...although, again, it would have been nice to exercise a little independence. Not to mention, use the morning to meet back up with Veronica and figure out our next steps.

We *had* to be getting close to the moment we would descend down into the Catacombs to find the hidden chamber. I couldn't tell if I was nervous or excited about that.

It was another beautifully sunny day in Paris, but even the backdrop of the Eiffel Tower in the distance behind us wasn't enough to distract me from finding the hidden chamber.

"I have something for you, sweetie," said Dad, breaking through my thoughts.

"Hmm?"

Dad pulled out a small patch with an image of the Eiffel Tower embroidered on it. "It's for your backpack. I thought you might like to have another."

I took it from his outstretched hand and ran my fingers over the stitching. My eyes began to water just a bit. The first patch on my purple backpack was from my mom, who had visited France for a lecture when I was little. It made me realize how much I missed her.

"Thanks, Dad, I love it."

"Everything okay, Harley? You've barely had a bite," Dad said, eyeing me suspiciously. I was usually a pretty good eater.

"Hm? Oh yeah, I'm fine, just fine," I said, taking an absent-minded bite. Daisy nudged my leg for some scraps since I clearly wasn't going to finish my breakfast.

"Well, I'd eat up. You're going to need energy for what I have in mind this morning," he said, sipping his coffee loudly.

"And what would that be?" I asked.

He smirked at me. "How about a tour of the legendary Catacombs?"

My stomach twisted in quick knots. What were the odds he'd suggest the Catacombs of all things? If only he knew I'd be getting my own tour of them soon enough.

"You do know about the Catacombs, don't you?" he asked, taking my pause for confusion.

I decided to play it cool. Just in case he might be onto me. "Not a lot. It's a giant network of tunnels below the city, right?" I asked.

He nodded enthusiastically. "Right. But there's more to them than that. I was reading up on them. Did you know that to this day, people *still* go missing in those tunnels every year? Even when they're warned not to go wandering off?"

"What do you mean by people 'still' go missing?" I asked, a chill creeping up my spine.

He wiped his mouth with a napkin and folded it. "People have been disappearing down in the Catacombs for hundreds of years. My favorite legend is one from the French Revolution era in the late 1700s. Apparently, a Monsieur Philibert Aspairt served as the butler to a particularly wealthy family. During a dinner party one night, he went down into their wine cellar and somehow discovered a secret entrance to the Catacombs. The poor butler decided to check it out, only to have his candle go out, throwing him into complete darkness."

I knew how that felt.

"He got confused and became utterly lost trying to navigate the tunnels and find his way out," Dad continued. "He never came back, and nobody at the estate ever knew what happened to him. Not until they found his body fifty years later when that part of the Catacombs was excavated."

Then he leaned over the table like he was whispering a secret to me. "They buried him right where they found him, and they say that to this day, his ghost continues to haunt the Catacombs. Sometimes, you can hear his cries for help echoing through the tunnels."

My eyes grew wide as the knots in my stomach unclenched, only to clench even tighter than before.

"Dad! Stop trying to scare me," I said, trying to untie the knots in my stomach.

Dad laughed lightly. "Don't worry, it's just a story. Probably made up to spook tourists like us."

His cell phone rang loudly from inside his chest pocket. He

slipped it out and looked at the screen. "Sorry, it's the dig site manager. Give me a second," he said and went inside to answer.

Now I was *definitely* too distracted to finish my breakfast. Veronica never mentioned anything about ghosts in the Catacombs!

I wasn't sure which was worse: coming face to face with ghosts or with the revived skeletons of who those ghosts once were. I'd prefer neither, which meant Veronica and I still had a job to do—whether the legends were true or not.

But how was I supposed to help her with that job if I couldn't get a moment to slip away?

Dad reemerged on the balcony, no longer on his phone but with his laptop open in his hands. "Apparently, there's a mountain of paperwork for the dig that wasn't filled out correctly. And the person usually in charge of that stuff is still out sick. So that leaves this emergency up to me to fix," he said. "Sorry, Harley, I'm afraid the Catacombs will have to wait."

Maybe for you at least, I thought but didn't dare say out loud.

"That's okay. I'll take Daisy for a walk instead. Get us both out of your hair," I told him, secretly slipping the last half of my croissant to a very grateful Daisy. Now was my chance to meet back up with Veronica.

"Sure, but don't go wandering too far, okay?" Dad said, barely looking up from his computer. "This is a big city to get lost in. Catacombs or no Catacombs."

It felt like we were right back in our early days of traveling the world together, with me eager to explore on my own and Dad keeping a tight grip on my every move. This Paris trip was very far from everything it was initially supposed to be. In just about every way.

"I'll be fine, Dad, don't worry," I told him as I hooked Daisy up to her leash. "I'm not a little kid anymore. I can spend a morning or two on my own from time to time, y'know."

But he was already too immersed in his work to hear me.

So I grabbed my backpack and was already texting Veronica as Daisy and I left the hotel room.

Chapter 11
Home Not-So-Sweet Home

"We're *still* not ready to find the chamber?" I asked Veronica as the two of us, plus Daisy, crossed the busy street. "But we have the map and the key. Since we're not planning on bringing any skeletons back to life, what else do we need?"

Veronica was wearing her signature red beret and ballet flats. She held a bag of freshly baked baguettes in her hands that smelled as if they had just been pulled out of the oven.

We were headed for the Paris Metro, an underground line of train systems connecting the entire city. It sounded awfully similar to the Catacombs to me. Only a lot more convenient.

"I know, but I believe it is important for us to gather as much information as we can before we go down there," Veronica explained as we descended a stairwell dipping down into a Metro entrance from the sidewalk. I could hear the screeching and groaning of the trains coming and going below.

"Is it true that someone gets lost in the Catacombs every year?" I asked, feeling my stomach clench again. The thought of roaming through the dark tunnels without a way out was terrifying.

"Not every year, but it happens more than people think," she said. "I think we should talk to someone who has spent a lot of time in the Catacombs. So that we understand what—and who—we might really be up against."

After a completely confusing twenty-minute ride through the tunnels of the Metro, we got off at a station on the outskirts of Paris. I could tell Daisy was thankful to be back above ground and out of the city.

Here, there were fewer sprawling buildings constructed in an interconnected grid and many more free-standing homes. The neighborhood we were walking through was pretty swanky. The homes lining the streets were big and old but well-kept, with neat little rows of potted trees and flowers in front of each one.

Except for the one we finally stopped at.

It was another big, old house, but this one was actually showing its age. Because someone had clearly stopped caring for it a long time ago.

"What is this place?" I asked Veronica. It looked like a haunted house.

Why was everything about this morning in particular already so spooky?

The once-white side paneling was now brown and gray in most areas. The roof sagged slightly on one side. Most of the windows had been broken and boarded up with spare pieces of plywood. And the front garden was so overgrown with weeds that you could barely see the cracked concrete path leading up to the faded red front door.

"This is the home of Mario Costa. One of the most famous explorers of the Paris Catacombs," Veronica said, standing next to me and staring up at the old house. She looked as nervous as I felt. "I thought if anyone could help us prepare for our journey to the secret chamber, it would be him." She looked down at the map she had opened on her phone and then back up at the house. "Although I will admit, this is not what I expected to find when we got here. He was once very famous. And very wealthy. I wonder what has gone wrong."

"Do you think he will help us?"

Veronica shrugged. "I hope so. Mario has been a dear friend of my family since before I was born. He used to tell me stories of the catacombs when I was a little girl." She flicked a strand of black hair from her eyes. "But he's become a bit reclusive over the last few years. We haven't seen much of him."

Before we could change our minds about a visit with this Mario Costa, the house's front door creaked open just a crack. "*Qu'est-ce que tu veux?*" a raspy voice said slowly from somewhere beyond the gap.

"Please, we just wish to ask you some questions," Veronica responded in English. I wondered why if the person had specifically spoken French. "And we brought some fresh baguettes."

She gingerly held the bag up to him.

"No. Go away," the voice responded harshly back, now in English. But his accent was thick and not like when other French people spoke English. There was something different about it I couldn't pinpoint.

Then Veronica spoke a whole string of words in a rapid language that I *knew* wasn't French. But I wasn't sure what other language it was.

What was going on?

There was a pause from the opening in the doorway. Finally, the door creaked open enough for us to get a glimpse of Mario Costa.

By my deduction, he was at least in his sixties, though he could have been much older. It was hard to tell because, much like his home, he was very unkempt.

His graying hair was shaggy and hanging nearly to his shoulders, and his matching gray beard stubble was growing in thick and patchy. The bags under his brown eyes were deep, just like the wrinkles in his forehead that appeared as he squinted at us. Even though the day was warm, he wore a stained, dark green sweatshirt and was still in his striped pajama pants. I wondered if we had interrupted him in the middle of a nap.

"I will give you five minutes," he said in that same thick accent. He snatched the bag of baguettes from Veronica's hand. Then he walked away from his front door, leaving it open for us to follow.

"What was all that about?" I whispered to Veronica as we walked up the stone pathway to the door.

"Mario is originally from Italy. He taught me some Italian when I was a kid," she explained.

I was impressed. Veronica could speak three languages—that I currently knew of—to my one and a half. I did learn a bit of Latin from one of my tutors.

If I wanted to become a seasoned S.M.A.L.L. agent like her, I really needed to up my game.

Daisy, eager to escape the heat outside, pulled against her leash and through the front door first. "Easy, girl, be polite," I told her as we followed her.

But it really wasn't any cooler in the house than it was outside.

In fact, the foyer that we stepped into felt kind of damp with warmth. Like the room was sweating just as much as we were.

Several parts of the graying walls had clearly sprung leaks at some point in their past and were now dotted with old water stains. Both the ceiling and the floor were cracked and warped in enough places that I wondered if it was safe to walk around.

And the living room to the right of the foyer, where Mario had wandered into, was filled with furniture that was so old and sagging, I was concerned when he plopped himself down onto the couch. But it held his weight, emitting nothing but a loud groan and a plume of dust.

I hoped Veronica was right about Mario Costa.

CHAPTER 12
A TROUBLED PAST

Mario motioned to two ripped and faded armchairs across from him. But we stood motionless between the foyer and the living room, weighing our options. I wasn't thrilled about the idea of sitting in this strange old house with an even stranger—and maybe even older—man. Even if he was supposedly an expert on the Catacombs.

But Daisy didn't give me much choice when she wiggled her leash from my grasp and went bounding across the living room for Mario. She yipped happily as she leaped right into his lap on the couch.

"Daisy, no! Off the furniture!" I told her. Though she was allowed on the furniture in our house back in the United States, I'd been taught to keep her off furniture in other people's homes. It was the polite thing to do.

Mario stared down in bewilderment at the little dog in his lap, who was wagging her tail something fierce and staring right back. Then he looked up at Veronica and me and suddenly burst out laughing.

We weren't sure what to make of it.

"You are worried about the furniture?" Mario finally asked after catching his breath. "*This* furniture?" He gestured around the room. Then he laughed again and scratched Daisy right behind the ears, just where she liked it. She seemed completely content.

If Daisy could trust Mario enough to be comfortable, I supposed we could too. So when he motioned for us to have a seat again, we took him up on his offer.

The armchairs were actually a lot comfier than they looked. And smelled.

"Thank you so much for agreeing to speak to us," Veronica began.

"Bah, it's fine," he responded, waving his hand. "You've grown up."

Veronica shrugged. "Well, it's been a while since we've seen each other. My parents send their best."

Mario nodded, said nothing. Veronica continued. "Thank you again for seeing us. We just wanted to know what the Catacombs are like. You know them better than anyone."

He nodded slowly, letting Daisy lick at one of the stains on his shirt. "If you want to know the Catacombs, why do you not simply take a public tour?" he asked.

"Because we're not interested in the part of the Catacombs the public tours have to offer," I chimed in. I glanced at Veronica, wondering how much it was okay to give away. She nodded slightly for me to go on. "We want to know about some of the...deeper chambers," I told him.

Mario squinted at us again, those deep creases returning to his forehead. "Did Monet send you?"

"Of course not," said Veronica.

"Sorry, who?" I asked, turning my gaze on her.

Mario stopped petting Daisy and slumped back into the couch. She jumped from his lap and came to sit between Veronica and me.

"Albert Monet," Mario said.

I still had no idea who he was talking about.

"Wait a minute...you do not mean *the* Albert Monet, do you? Of the old Monet family line?" Veronica asked him. Her eyes were just about as wide as I'd ever seen them.

"Do you know of any other Monet family as well-known as his?" Mario questioned right back.

Veronica shook her head. "I suppose not. I am just not sure why you think we would be associated with him."

"Can someone please catch me up on what we're talking about?" I pleaded.

"The Monet family is one of the oldest families in France," Veronica explained. "Much like mine. Though, as I remember, there was some kind of mishap between them and the French government. I thought they had all left France for different parts of the world."

Mario snorted. "That is what he *wants* people to think. But no, Monsieur Albert Monet has been here all these years. Working behind the scenes, using those with power and wealth to his advantage, attempting to reestablish his family name." Then he leaned forward, his expression turning grave. "Working with children is not his style, so I believe you are not with him. And that is good. You would do well to steer clear of him and his entire family line."

Something didn't add up to me. If this Albert Monet only wanted to associate with people of class and wealth, then what was he doing apparently scaring the pants off a tired old man like Mario?

"Is that what he did to you?" I asked Mario cautiously. "Take advantage of you in some way?"

After a few moments of pause, Mario finally nodded. "You are not unwise in coming to ask me questions about the Catacombs.

No one knows them like I do. I have ventured further into those tunnels and chambers than anyone else. At least further than anyone who was still able to find their way back above ground." He picked absentmindedly at his dirty fingernails as he thought of the past.

Veronica leaned forward in her chair. "In all your travels down there, did you ever come across a door you could not open?" she asked. "A door with a massive, round stone blocking the entrance?"

Mario nodded again. "Albert came asking me the same question several years ago. Told me that if I could lead him to that stone doorway, he would spare my life when he brought destruction upon the world that had wronged him."

I *really* didn't like the sound of this Albert Monet guy. But unfortunately, I was beginning to connect the dots. The dots that started to show exactly what we might be up against.

"Naturally, I told him that if what he said about the chamber *was* true, why would I ever help him seek it out?" Mario continued. "He may be bitter about his history with this city and this country, but I certainly still enjoy it." He hung his head then. "Or at least, I used to."

Daisy whined sadly from where she sat at my feet. I felt sorry for Mario too. Whatever Albert had done to him had clearly taken a toll. If I had to guess, it'd been quite a few years since Mario had even left his house. How scared did someone have to be to never go anywhere?

If he had that much reason to be afraid of Albert Monet...then we did too.

"So it must be Albert Monet who has stolen the Rose de France," Veronica said.

I nodded. Exactly. The Rose de France was the key to opening the inner tombs of the catacombs.

"But it would seem he still has not figured out how to get to the chamber." Veronica looked over at me as she spoke. "Or get it open."

"And it needs to stay that way," Mario told her, suddenly becoming anxious. "It has taken all my energy to stand against his threats all these years. You girls *must* drop this. Now. He is too dangerous to get involved with."

Then he stood quickly and went back to the front door, pulling it open for us. Clearly, the conversation was over.

I had about a million more questions to ask but didn't want to push Mario any further. The shadows under his eyes already seemed a shade darker than when we arrived.

Which only left one question for Veronica and me: What would Albert Monet do when he discovered we were trying to stop his plans?

CHAPTER 13
PRESERVE, PROTECT, PERSEVERE

"I cannot do this. We cannot do this. What do we do?"

Veronica was walking slightly ahead of me through the neighborhood away from Mario Costa's house. She was shaking her head and twisting her fingers around the S.M.A.L.L. medallion at the end of her necklace. It was the first time since we met that I had seen her truly flustered.

Once again, Daisy and I had to speed walk to keep up with her.

"Wait up, Veronica! Just hold on a minute!" I called out. Finally, she stopped walking.

"We must communicate with S.M.A.L.L. about Albert Monet. About what we face," she told me quickly. "They will give us a new mission when they understand what is going on."

A new mission? Without completing the one we already had? Was that something S.M.A.L.L. would even agree to do?

"Let's slow down and think about this for a second," I told her, trying to act calmer than I felt. Mario's story about Albert Monet had spooked me too. But there were a few essential facts to remember. "As far as we know, this Monet guy probably has the Rose de

France," I reminded her. "But he doesn't have the map to the chamber. And he also doesn't have the key to get in. Right?"

Veronica nodded, gently touching the necklace that was still safely sitting against her chest. The purple and white stone glistened in the late morning sunshine.

"We have everything we need to perform our own ritual to keep the bones at rest. He only has one of three things he needs to bring them to life. The odds are on our side," I continued. "Now, we just need to keep things that way."

Veronica's green eyes sparkled as she stared at the stone key around her neck.

"You are right, Harley James," she finally said with a soft smile. "Thank you."

"For what?"

"For reminding me what it means to be an agent of S.M.A.L.L."

I smiled back. "*Preserve. Protect. Persevere.* Right?"

"Right."

Feeling at least a little better about the challenges ahead, we headed back for the Paris Metro. My tour group's free morning to explore was just about up, and I also owed my dad a check-in.

It was finally time to make our way to the Catacombs together and find that hidden chamber. We had to do it soon before Albert Monet got any wiser about what we were up to.

We agreed to meet up tonight after my dad and the chaperone had gone to bed. Hopefully, we'd make it into the chamber, do the ritual, and be back out before breakfast tomorrow.

We rode the Metro back to the stop near my hotel. The train was packed to the brim nearly the whole ride, and the platform wasn't any less busy to navigate. Both Veronica and I bumped up against quite a few people as we fought our way to the stairs leading back above ground.

"Remember, nine o'clock tonight," Veronica reminded me before we parted ways.

"Nine o'clock," I repeated. After a busy day of touring, everyone else would surely be asleep by then. Sneaking out to head to the Catacombs should be easy enough.

Daisy and I were just walking through the front door of my dad's hotel when my cell phone started ringing. It was Veronica. Was she changing her mind already? Did she need another pep talk?

"Everything okay?" I asked as I answered her call.

"No, Harley, no! Everything is not okay!"

I could hear the panic in her voice. "Why? What's going on?"

"My pendant is gone! The key to the chamber...it is missing!"

I froze in the middle of the hotel lobby. "What do you mean it's missing? I was just with you. I just saw it hanging on your necklace!"

"Someone must have cut it from my chain. I looked down, and the chain was there, but the pendant was gone. I retraced my steps back to the Metro, but it was nowhere to be found. Harley, do you think..." She trailed off.

But I knew exactly what she was about to ask.

"Unfortunately, Veronica, I do. I do think Albert Monet has finally caught on to us. And he was somewhere on that train or at that station, waiting for his chance." My stomach was doing that thing again where it gets all twisted into uncomfortable knots.

"But that means he now has two of the three items he needs for the ritual," Veronica said, her voice falling. "What do we do?"

We didn't have any other choice. We had a mission to complete.

"It means we have to make sure we stop him. Whatever it takes."

CHAPTER 14
SPILLING THE BEANS

Albert Monet still doesn't have the map. He still doesn't know how to get to the hidden chamber, I reminded myself as I punched the button for the hotel elevator.

But how long would it be before he figured out where the map was? Just like Veronica and I did?

Even though I still didn't know much about Monet, I got the sense that it wouldn't be very long at all.

That meant, key or no key, Veronica and I still needed to make our way to the chamber. If we could beat him there, maybe we could keep him from entering. I wasn't sure how, but there *had* to be a way. The fate of a lot of people depended on it.

The elevator doors finally opened, and Dad nearly ran smack into me as he rushed through them.

"Harley! Where have you been? I was just coming to look for you," he said, smoothing his curly hair.

"Out walking Daisy, like I said I'd be," I told him. Again, it wasn't exactly a lie...

"Well, you were gone *way* too long. I didn't know what happened to you."

I glanced down at the time on my phone. I had been gone less than an hour. And he was this freaked out?

"Dad, you know that if I had come to Paris on my own like originally planned, I would have been going a whole lot more than an hour between check-ins with you...right?" I asked him.

He frowned at me. "Well, you didn't come to Paris on your own after all, so that point is irrelevant," he responded as he led Daisy and me back across the hotel lobby.

I don't know if it was just bad timing with Veronica's necklace being stolen or if it was the build-up of losing my independence over the last few days, but I could feel anger and annoyance rising in me. It was making my chest and my cheeks feel warm.

I came to a halt just inside the hotel doors.

Dad was confused. "What wrong? It's time to meet up with our group," he said.

I couldn't help it. "*Our* group?" I asked him. "Dad, this was supposed to be *my* group. *My* trip to Paris. *My* chance to practice being independent. You said so yourself!"

Daisy whined as she watched me fight to hold back frustrated tears.

"Harley, I—" he started to say, but I cut him off.

"I love traveling the world with you, Dad. I really do. But I'm not a little kid anymore. I don't need you holding my hand every time we visit a new city." I sniffled. "You need to give me space to take care of myself." I couldn't bring myself to look up at him, but I heard him exhale loudly. And then I felt him place a gentle hand on my shoulder.

"Ah geez, Harley. I had no idea you felt that way. I'm really sorry," he said.

I finally looked up and into his sparkling green eyes that

matched mine. They really were full of apologies. But also something else.

It was sadness.

He removed his hand from my shoulder and put it in his pocket instead. "Listen, you go and meet up with your group, okay? It's probably about time I head back to the dig site anyways," he told me.

"You don't have to leave Paris. I just meant—"

But he held up his other hand to stop me. "It's okay, Harley. You've explained enough. I get it. I'll give you space." Then he started back for the elevator. "Just promise me you'll check in every once in a while. Just so I know you and Daisy are all right," he said as the elevator doors opened and a young couple stepped out. He took their place inside. "See you in a few days."

Then the doors closed, and that was that.

I felt a lump form in my throat. I hadn't meant to make him so upset. But I really *did* need some space.

S.M.A.L.L. needed me. I had a mission to complete. One that would save the people of Paris from a dark future.

And if I was being honest, it'd be much easier to sneak away from just the chaperone—rather than the chaperone and my dad—to venture down into the Catacombs.

"Come on, Daisy, let's go. He'll be okay," I told her. "We'll explain everything to him once this whole ordeal is over for good."

But even as I said the words, I couldn't be quite sure exactly how this whole thing would end or if I'd even get the chance I needed to tell my dad what was really going on.

CHAPTER 15
HIGH STAKES AND STOMACHACHES

I met back up with my tour group, just in time for Madame Fleur to announce we'd finally be visiting the Eiffel Tower today.

I smiled. *Been there, done that.*

By the time we started walking, Veronica had sent me three text messages back-to-back.

The first one said: *"I think we need to go to the chamber as soon as possible."*

She was already on the same page I was.

The second text said: *"Can you send me the pictures you took of the map?"*

The third one said: *"I will plan our route while you figure out how to meet up with me."*

That was a good idea. No one but Mario Costa knew more about navigating the Catacomb tunnels than Veronica and her family did. Her ancestors had spent decades traveling through those tunnels to meet up with other families of France in secret. Veronica had even known exactly where to go to get us right outside the

Hôtel national des Invalides when we first entered one of the Catacomb tunnels together.

If anyone could decipher that map and get us to the chamber before Albert Monet, it was her.

I swiped open my phone and sent her all the pictures of the chamber map I had snapped back inside the secret room of the Musée des Plans-Reliefs. Then I climbed onto the tour bus with the rest of the group.

We had barely started down the street when my phone pinged with another text from Veronica: *"One of the tunnels on the map leads directly through the Catacombs tourist area."*

What did that mean?

As though somehow reading my mind, she followed up with another text: *"That means we will have to wait until they are closed at 7pm. So there will be no one around to stop us."*

I texted her back: *"7 o'clock then?"*

It was a while before she texted back. We were nearly to Champ de Mars, the park where the Eiffel Tower stood, before my phone finally pinged again. Loads of tourists were buzzing around the base of the tower like a swarm of honeybees. I watched them silently, wondering how many of them knew what lay beneath the cobbled path under their feet.

Hopefully, I would do my job and they'd never find out.

My phone beeped. It was a text from Veronica.

"Yes. 7 o'clock. I only hope we will not be too late."

I did too.

"THE EIFFEL TOWER was built to be one of the main attractions at the Paris World's Fair in 1889. Its focus was the vast constructions in iron and steel that were the great industrial advancement of that time..."

Our tour guide rattled on about the history of the Eiffel Tower. I had been looking forward to learning more about Paris's iconic centerpiece, but right now it was hard to concentrate.

My mind was swirling with thoughts of the Catacombs, Albert Monet, Veronica, ancient treasures with incredible powers, and of course, Dad.

Though I should have been focusing on coming up with a plan for stopping Monet, I found my thoughts drifting back to wondering what Dad was doing at that moment. Was he already headed back to the French countryside? Was he already digging through the dirt on his hands and knees? Or was he still working his way through that pile of paperwork he had to finish? Whatever it was, I hoped he wasn't feeling too sad. And I hoped he wouldn't be upset with me forever.

Before I knew it, our day of touring was rounding down toward dinnertime. I'd saved just enough room in my brain throughout the day to think about a plan to sneak away that evening undetected. I knew that I needed to put the wheels in motion now.

We ate dinner at a local restaurant that served mountainous bowls of pasta topped with rich, decadent sauces. It was delicious, and I was surprised at how hungry I was, scarfing nearly a whole bowl down. My plan had been to tell the chaperone after dinner that I was feeling sick so that I could pretend to spend the evening alone in my room unbothered, then sneak out just before seven to meet up with Veronica.

But the truth was, eating that whole bowl of pasta *did* make my stomach a little upset. That, or the nerves I felt as my trip to the Catacombs loomed closer were getting to me. Either way, the chaperone was kind enough to escort me back to the hotel and make sure

I was comfortably tucked in for the night. She'd be back to check on me first thing in the morning.

The second she closed my door, I leaped back out of bed, changed into a fresh pair of jeans and a jacket, and stuffed my purple backpack with all the things I could possibly think I might need for a dark journey through a winding maze.

Then it was 6:55 and time to go.

"You ready for this, Daisy?" I asked. She cocked her head and stared up at me with confused brown eyes. "Yeah, I'm not sure either," I confessed as we tiptoed from our room.

Five minutes and a few blocks later, I arrived near the Eiffel Tower, where Veronica and I had first met. I slid the puzzle pieces on the ground back into the image of the French symbol of peace, and the ground opened up again. I headed down the ramp with Daisy, clicking on a flashlight I had thought to bring with me this time. And I didn't scream when my beam of light lit up Veronica's face waiting for me in the dark this time.

"Ready to go?" she asked, clicking on her own flashlight.

I shivered as the air in the tight tunnel around us suddenly seemed to change. "Ready," I barely managed to squeak out.

With that, we began our descent down into the Catacombs of Paris.

CHAPTER 16
SMALL SOLUTIONS AND BIG PROBLEMS

We walked in silence for a while, the only sound our shoes squelching on the wet limestone beneath our feet and the drip, drip, drip of sewage water coming down the walls. The ceiling was just a few feet above my head. I could practically feel the spiders and centipedes crawling on my skin.

The dampness in the air seemed to wrap itself around my shoulders and down my throat. I tried to focus on the words of S.M.A.L.L.: *Preserve. Protect. Persevere.*

This was definitely a persevere moment for me.

Eventually, we came to a familiar fork in the tunnel. The right side sloped up back toward the surface. The left side descended deeper into darkness.

This time, Veronica headed left.

I could feel my ears popping as the pressure changed. That's how far and fast we were dropping further and further away from the city above our heads. Soon, there was no more moisture on the walls or floor. Just a long, dark tunnel stretching ahead for what seemed like forever.

I really hoped we weren't about to come face to face with any ghosts. Not that I *really* believed in that stuff. Though, with how many ancient legends I had recently learned were true, I could never be sure.

"This tunnel should lead us into the main chamber of the tourist entrance to the Catacombs," Veronica said, finally breaking the silence. "From there is the only access point to a tunnel that will take us where we need to go."

"But what are we going to do when we get there? To the chamber?" I asked. I hoped she had come up with some kind of plan during the day because I sure hadn't.

"I am still figuring that part out," she said. "We will have to see what we find when we get there."

After another few minutes, the small tunnel leveled out. Then it ended abruptly at a set of stone stairs carved into the wall.

Veronica double-checked the map on her phone. "Yes, this is right," she assured me, then started up the stairs. I let Daisy follow up after her, then I brought up the rear.

But the stairs seemed to lead to nowhere. After ten steps they just ended, right up against a ceiling of dirt and rock.

"This cannot be correct," Veronica said, consulting the map again. "This is the way. It must be."

I scooted around her and stared at the ceiling, sweeping my flashlight's beam across it. Near the top step, the light caught...something. It was a little circle carved into the rock. It looked familiar.

"Hey, can I see the map for a minute?" I asked Veronica. She handed her phone over, and I pinched and zoomed in on the screen to the upper right corner of the map, where a strange symbol consisting of a circle with four squiggly lines across it was drawn.

I looked up at the rock above my head and rubbed my thumb against it. A little bit of built-up dust fell away to reveal the same four squiggly lines drawn across this circle too. Then I rubbed it a little too hard, and my thumb pushed it up into the rock surrounding it.

Oops.

A horrible grinding noise started somewhere above our heads. Suddenly, a square section of the ceiling rock cracked away from the stone around it, dropping dust and dirt onto us. We both ducked and shielded our faces with our hands. I reached a hand down to help Daisy shield her eyes too.

After a minute, when the grinding and dirt shower seemed to be over, I peeked through my hands to see a gaping hole where the section of rock had once been. Through it, on the other side, was a large, open cavern.

"How did you know to do that?" Veronica asked, bewildered.

I pointed to the small circle carved into the ceiling, then showed her the map on the phone. "The symbols. They match. See?" I said. I didn't tell her that I hadn't actually expected the ceiling to disappear when I just touched the thing.

"Of course," Veronica said. "That is the symbol of the Rose de France. I bet we will find more of them throughout the Catacombs!"

"Is that so?" a strange voice suddenly answered.

Veronica and I both froze, and Daisy growled deeply.

Through the open hole above us, a man appeared. His body was big, round, and adorned in a fancy, dark blue suit. His matching round face was pale, with small glasses perched on the edge of a crooked nose. His brown hair was slicked back away from his face, and matching brown hair was trimmed into a neat goatee around his mouth. His crocodile teeth, which were as crooked as his nose, sneered down at us as he spoke again.

"My, my, my, if it isn't Mademoiselle Veronica Rousseau. And her little friend."

Daisy barked up at the man angrily.

"*Et une chienne?*" the man said, looking down at Daisy with confusion. "Why in the world would you bring a dog into the Catacombs?"

But Veronica ignored his question. "How do you know my name?" she asked instead.

The man sneered down at us again, and I didn't like the look in his cold, deep brown eyes.

"I know much more than your name, child," he said.

Now I didn't like the look crossing Veronica's face either.

"Then maybe you should tell us your name. So we can all be familiar," Veronica said right back. It was almost like she was taunting him, and I wasn't sure why.

The man threw his head back and bellowed out a short laugh. "Very well," he finally said. "We'll play your way…for now. My name is Albert Monet."

CHAPTER 17
NO WAY OUT

Before I even had a moment to digest the sudden danger we were in, two pairs of long, strong arms reached down through the hole above us and grasped our shoulders firmly. Veronica and I were yanked off our feet and through the hole, leaving Daisy down in the tunnel below.

But no matter how hard I kicked and squirmed, whoever held onto me didn't loosen their grip. And as I was finally planted firmly back on my feet, I saw why.

Albert Monet had two men assisting him in the Catacombs this evening. Or more like two henchmen, to be exact. They were tall, broad, and rippling with muscles throughout every inch of their bodies. They had to be twins because even their buzzed blond haircuts looked identical.

"Let go of me!" Veronica demanded, squirming just as much as I was. Monet's thugs didn't say a word but eventually loosened their grips.

That's when I finally looked around the room we had been pulled into. It was large and circular, filled with soft yellow light hanging from the ceiling and long iron torches lining the walls that looked like they hadn't been lit in a long time and were more for decoration. There was also a wide stone staircase behind us leading up and away from the room and informational signs posted everywhere in various languages.

But the most striking feature of all was the towering wall of human bones lining the other side of the cavern. Skulls with gaping sockets were stacked by the hundreds. The spaces between them were filled with what were probably femurs and fibulas, the only other human bones I could think of at the moment. My brain was too stunned to do much else.

This had to be the main tourist area of the Catacombs. Just like Veronica had said we'd come across on our way to the hidden chamber.

Daisy started barking from below, snapping me out of my creeped-out trance. I sank to my knees and reached back through the hole. "Come on, Daisy, come here!" I called to her.

"Ah, ah, ah," Monet sounded, snapping his fingers. One of his henchmen quickly pulled me away from the hole and Daisy. "I do not feel like taking a dog for a walk tonight," Monet said.

"You can't just leave her there!" I yelled at him. "She'll get lost!"

"We will all get lost if you two do not cooperate," he hissed back, turning away from us. With a wave of his hand, he sent his other henchman sliding the stone slab back over the hole, drowning out Daisy's barking.

"Stay there, Daisy. We'll come back for you!" I yelled through the floor, hoping she could hear me. And hoping what I was telling her was true. I had no idea how this night was about to turn out now.

"You may come back for her only after you help me," Monet said as he crossed the room, headed for the wall of bones.

"And why would we do that?" Veronica challenged him. Wow, she was acting a whole lot braver than I felt at the moment.

"Because if you don't, I will never let you leave the Catacombs." His words echoed around the chamber menacingly, reminding us of just how vast these chambers and tunnels really were.

"Why are you doing this? Why do you want to raise the dead?" Veronica tried again.

Monet whirled around to stare her down. "As a member of one of the oldest families in France, you must understand what it means to feel important. To have the superiority and power that comes with that importance," he said to her.

But Veronica shook her head. "My family has always been content with living a quiet life. Our role in the family history of France has always been one of service and protection."

Monet's brown eyes flared with frustration as he took in her words. "Then you cannot possibly understand what it means to *lose* all that power. To have it stripped away from you," he snarled at her. He calmly smoothed the front of his blue suit, then smoothed his already-perfect goatee. "Enough talking. It is time to find the chamber. I will perform the ritual tonight, and then all of France will be mine. After that, the world!"

He snapped his fingers again, and his henchmen jostled Veronica and me into walking toward a large tunnel opening across the room, away from the wall of bones (thank goodness).

The tunnel had an intimidating chain hanging across it and a big red sign hanging from the chain that said, "DO NOT ENTER."

The air seemed to grow thicker as we headed deeper underground. I tried to suck in a deep breath, but instead of relaxing me it made me cough. Veronica peered back at me and I nodded to her.

I'm okay, I mouthed to her. At least that's what I was telling myself at the moment.

Monet undid the chain and beckoned us to head into the tunnel first.

"I know you possess the map," he told us. "You will use it to guide us all to the chamber of the Rose de France. And your clever little friend will figure out each and every puzzle blocking our path as we make our way. If you do not—" He paused to reach into his deep suit pockets. From one, he pulled out Veronica's missing pendant, with the small purple and white stone. From the other, he pulled out another purple and white gem that looked almost *identical* to Veronica's, only much larger and almost perfectly round. I could see a missing section where Veronica's stone had apparently been carved from.

"—then I will simply destroy the Rose de France and the key," Monet finished. "Do you know what happens if they are destroyed?"

I shook my head no, but Veronica nodded. "The legend says that the Catacombs will crumble, taking the entire city of Paris down with it," she barely whispered.

I didn't know which was worse: millions of undead skeletons wreaking havoc on an entire country or one of the most important cities in the world falling to pieces.

We had no choice but to do as we were told.

.

CHAPTER 18
THE WRITING ON THE WALL

I stepped into the new tunnel first. It was somehow instantly much darker than any tunnel I had been in with Veronica before. I clicked my flashlight back on, which cast just enough light to see the wall in front of me.

There, almost too small to see unless you knew to look for it, was another symbol of the Rose de France carved into the wall, right where it met the floor of the tunnel.

We were on the right track. But now, I wasn't sure if that was a good thing or a bad thing.

"Head down this tunnel, then take the first tunnel that comes up on your left, Harley," Veronica instructed me, her phone now back in her hands with the map open.

Monet and his two henchmen filed into the tunnel right behind her.

"Are you sure this is the right thing to do?" I whispered to Veronica as I walked. A burst of icy wind from somewhere deep within the tunnel hit me with full force, sending shivers all over my body.

She shrugged helplessly. "We have to play along, it's our only option," she whispered back. "Then maybe we can distract him long enough to stop this whole thing from happening."

This was a very different Veronica than I had seen back in the main tourist chamber a few minutes ago. She was more unsure of herself than she had been since I'd met her.

I understood how she felt. This was probably one of the worst situations I had ever found myself in since joining up with S.M.A.L.L.

Too late to change my membership status now.

Our group walked on in silence for a few minutes, passing lots of tunnels on the right side before the first tunnel on the left finally appeared. It was so much smaller than the tunnel we were currently in that I nearly missed it.

Veronica and I both had to stoop to head into this tunnel, and I wondered if Monet and his men would be able to fit. Unfortunately, they did and followed just as closely behind us.

"Follow this tunnel as far as it will take you. I believe we will reach our first puzzle where it dead-ends," Veronica told me.

It was a long walk, sloping downward most of the way. Again, numerous other tunnels appeared on the right and left sides of us as we went, but I kept straight. It was hard to tell exactly how long we walked, but it was long enough for my stooped back to start aching.

"Did you hear that?" Veronica suddenly whispered to me as she came to a halt.

I froze too. "Hear what?" I asked. I hadn't heard anything other than the shuffling footsteps of our group.

"Shhh," Veronica said, her eyes growing wide as she looked around. Not that there was much to see.

"What is the delay?" Monet grumbled from behind her.

"I thought I heard...voices," Veronica told him.

Even Monet paused for a worried moment. But then he shook

his head. "I hear nothing. There is no one down here but us. Keep moving," he said.

I continued walking but was stepping a little more cautiously now. If Veronica said she heard voices, then I believed her. What I *didn't* want to consider was that those voices might belong to the ghosts of lost butlers...

"The tunnel should end here," Veronica said after another few minutes. And she was right. From a distance, it looked like we had come to an abrupt end to the tunnel, with nothing to show for it. But as I got closer, I could see words carved into the wall and a pile of what looked like small stones on the ground in front of it.

But they weren't stones. They were small, square tiles, each with a letter of the alphabet on its front. And in the wall above them were five notches side by side, the exact size and shape of the tiles.

And above that, carved into the wall, was a riddle.

> Je commence et termine avec 500.
> Je garde un 5 au milieu.
> Je suis incomplet sans la toute première lettre.
> Je suis incomplet sans le tout premier numéro.
> Je suis un homme, mais quel est mon nom?

Veronica looked at me, waiting, but I gave her a small shrug.

"I don't speak French."

"Oh right," she said. "It says: *I start and end with 500. I keep a 5 in my middle. I am incomplete without the very first letter. I am incomplete without the very first number. I am a man, but what is my name?*"

Clearly, you were supposed to select the correct tiles to put into the right places in the wall.

I pulled out my notebook and jotted the riddle down and then stared at the lines. This had to be one of the most confusing riddles I had ever seen in my life. Numbers and letters that added up to a man's name? There weren't even any numbers in the pile of tiles, as far as I could see. So how did that make any sense?

I looked to Veronica for help, but she looked even more puzzled than me. "Can you solve it?" she asked.

"I'm not sure."

Behind us, Monet was already getting impatient. "What is the hold-up? Get to work," he barked at me.

I didn't always do so well with puzzles under pressure. But I had to try.

First, I sorted through the tiles at my feet and confirmed there were no number tiles to be seen. Only capitalized letters of the alphabet. So, this "man's name" would still be composed of five regular letters.

Okay...so what letters can be used as numbers too? I asked myself. Maybe the letter "O" was a pretty good place to start. It looked just like the number zero. But as I read the lines of the riddle over and over again, the letter "O" didn't seem to fit.

"What letters are also numbers?" I asked Veronica, suddenly drawing a blank. "Besides the letter 'O,' can you think of any letters of the alphabet that also look like a number?"

Veronica tapped her flashlight against her lip in thought. "How about the letter 'I'? Does it not also look like the number one?" she asked.

And just like that, it all suddenly fell into place.

"Brilliant!" I shouted, which was much too loud as it bounced around our tiny tunnel.

The letter "I" was also used for the Roman numeral 1. This man's name was made up of letters of the alphabet that were also Roman numerals!

I started sifting through the tiles, finding the exact five I was looking for.

The name started and ended with 500—in Roman numerals, which was represented by the letter "D." I grabbed two of those.

A 5 was in the middle, which was the Roman numeral "V."

Then, the first letter of the alphabet, "A," and the first numerical number, "I," took the last two spots.

One by one, I placed my carefully selected tiles into their corresponding notches on the wall to spell out the name:

DAVID

The moment the last tile clicked into place, the wall in front of us began to grind and groan, just like the hatch to the tourist cavern had. Small blasts of dust puffed out from the seams of what appeared to be a rectangular door, cut into the stone wall.

We all watched with fascination as the wall slowly swung open to reveal a very peculiar cavern beyond it.

CHAPTER 19
A CLOSE CALL

"Is this it? Is this the chamber of the Rose de France?" Albert Monet asked as he brushed past us through the tunnel and into the new cavern that had appeared.

"No, we are not there yet," Veronica told him.

That was a relief. There was still time to try to figure out how we were going to stop Albert Monet from either bringing millions of skeletons to life or sending Paris crumbling into the depths of the Catacombs.

"Then what is this place?" Monet asked again.

"Just another part of the maze," she said as we all filed into the room.

It reminded me a bit of the tourist cavern, only much more dark and drab. And the smell? It was like walking into a room piled to the ceiling with sweaty gym socks.

The circular room was constructed of large, gray bricks covered in cobwebs and dust that had to be centuries old. And in the lining between each brick was set a long, slender bone.

I didn't want to look at the walls, so I focused on the center of the room instead. Which didn't turn out to be a better choice.

An old wooden chair sat atop a circular flat stone raised off the ground. And in the chair sat a full human skeleton, with its feet planted firmly on the ground and its arms resting on the chair's armrests. It looked so perfectly peaceful that I almost wondered if it was fake.

Doubt it.

Monet and his two henchmen, who had yet to say a single word since this whole escapade had begun, moved to the center of the room to examine our new friend. I took the opportunity to talk to Veronica privately.

"So, what's the plan now? How far are we taking this thing?" I whispered, hopeful that she now, finally, had a plan.

But she was distracted. Her eyes were darting up and around the room like she was looking for something. "You do not hear that?" she asked me again. "You do not hear voices whispering?"

I was very thankful to be able to tell her that I didn't. What had gotten into her? "Are you okay?" I asked. "I mean, of course, you're not okay, but you seem…less okay than usual."

She sighed. "I have not been entirely truthful with you, Harley," she said. "But you deserve to know the truth now. I was not S.M.A.L.L.'s first choice for this mission. They wanted a different agent to handle it."

That was surprising to hear. Veronica seemed like a great agent to me. "So why didn't they give it to someone else?" I asked.

"They almost did. Until I revealed that my family is the protector of the key. The key that I have now lost," she explained. She was holding back tears now. "Clearly, I was not the right choice for this mission after all. And I decided to drag you into it to help me. I am so sorry, Harley."

Before I could tell her that everything would be okay, that we would eventually figure this mess out and get out of the Catacombs, Monet was barking orders at us again.

"Mademoiselles! Your little meeting is over. Time for the next puzzle," he said with yet another finger snap. His cronies lumbered over to Veronica and me to shepherd us to the middle of the room.

I did my best not to look the skeleton directly in the face.

"See the symbol?" Monet asked, pointing to the pedestal the chair sat on. The small circle with squiggly lines was carved into the top of it. "So, what is the puzzle?" he asked me.

All I saw was a dusty chair and some old bones. It didn't seem like this was any sort of puzzle. But there was no denying the symbol of the Rose de France carved into the stone. That had to mean *something*.

The last time I touched one of these symbols, an unexpected hole had opened up. Maybe that was worth a try again.

I planted my thumb on the symbol and pushed it like an elevator button. Sure enough, it indented into the stone. But when I took my thumb away, I noticed something…off…about this symbol. Instead of the usual four squiggly lines across its surface, this one only had three.

I wonder what that could mean.

It didn't take long to find out.

The floor beneath us started to shake. Then the stone pedestal with the skeleton sitting on it slowly began to move backward. As it did, it left a gaping hole beneath it, growing wider and wider as the stone in the floor shifted. Through the hole, we saw an impossibly far drop into nothing but darkness.

But the floor didn't stop moving. It opened wider and wider, like a giant mouth trying to open up and swallow us whole. Veronica and I took a few steps back.

The chair with its skeleton wobbled on the edge of the hole for a few seconds before plummeting into darkness. A few seconds passed and then a minute, as I listened for it to hit the ground.

It fell so far that we never even heard it hit the bottom. A chill ran from my lower back all the way to my neck.

"Why is it not stopping?" Monet asked, just as confused as I was.

We were quickly backed up against the walls of the room. If the floor kept going like this, we'd have no more ground to stand on.

"I don't think that was the right button to push," I said, trying to keep my voice from trembling. "I think it was some kind of decoy."

"A what?" Veronica asked.

"A fake button. To throw us off the trail. Or get us into deeper trouble," I explained, not daring to gaze down at the drop below. My fear of heights was threatening to kick in.

Veronica quickly took her phone out of her pocket and brought up the map. "You are right, Harley. The map does not say to go down through the floor. It says to go…" she glanced around the room and pointed to the side nearly opposite where we were standing, "…there!"

The five of us wasted no time.

With what little floor there was left, we all sprinted around the perimeter of the room and to the opposite side, then started searching the wall for any sign of anything that could get us out of this mess.

The floor continued to grind and groan, widening with every second that passed. It was only a matter of time before we joined the skeleton's fate.

I ran my hands along the old stone, looking for the symbol. I came across one…but it had five squiggly lines instead of four! "Nobody touch that one!" I warned everyone. "Only press the symbol with four lines."

Everyone was running around the room now, frantically searching the walls for a clue. The hole in the floor was just about to reach us.

"I've got it!" Veronica finally shouted. She pressed a symbol above her head, nearly out of reach, and a slab of wall popped open to the right.

We all tumbled through the doorway just as the last of the floor in the previous room disappeared.

CHAPTER 20
WHEN PUZZLES CAUSE PROBLEMS

Our group tumbled into a brand-new tunnel. It was long and wide, stretching out into darkness ahead of us. The beams from our flashlights were scattered around the room, as we all scrambled back to our feet.

I placed my hands on my knees, breathing deeply. I glanced over at Veronica, who was holding onto her arm. There was small tear in her sleeve, and a few small streams of blood were running down her arm.

"Are you all right?"

"I'm fine," Veronica said, using a small scarf to wrap her wound. "It's just a scratch."

It looked like more than a scratch to me, but there wasn't much I could do to help. We had barely made it through the skeleton room.

If Veronica hadn't found that button at the last second...

I shivered, thinking about what would have happened to us.

"Please, Monet, we cannot go on," Veronica pleaded, looking just as shaken as me. "It is too dangerous."

But Albert Monet was paying her no attention. Instead, his eyes were glued to the Rose de France he had taken out of his pocket. It was about the size of a softball, and he cupped it with two hands, his eyes staring at it intently.

The stone was glowing.

"What does that mean?" I blurted out, not sure I wanted to know the answer.

Monet smiled crookedly. "It means we are not turning back. Because we are close to the chamber now."

He motioned us to follow him as his henchmen brought up the rear.

"The voices are getting louder," Veronica whispered to me as we walked.

I still heard nothing but our own footsteps and labored breathing as we all tried to get our nerves back under control.

"I have a bad feeling about this, Harley," she said. I nodded my head in agreement. The knots in my stomach were growing tighter. I opened my mouth to ask where we should go next, but one of Monet's men spoke instead.

"Over here," he said, pointing to a wall at the end of the tunnel. "I think I found something."

We moved along the tunnel carefully. I wondered if another giant hole was going to open up again and swallow us whole. The wall he was standing in front of was only about twenty feet ahead of us.

We all stopped and huddled around it, casting our flashlights in the same direction.

It was similar to the first puzzle in the way that it was carved into a wall blocking our way, and there was a pile of tiles on the floor in front of it.

But this one was a number puzzle. Each tile was triangular and had a single number on its surface. There were matching triangle shapes carved into the wall, some showing a number, some leaving a space for a tile to be inserted.

"Get going," Monet told me, stepping aside.

The numbers on the wall were arranged in a specific order to denote some kind of pattern I was supposed to follow:

$$3\ 5\ 8\ 13\ 22\ \_\ \_\ \_\ 137$$

AFTER I'D LOOKED over the sequence for a couple of minutes, it almost seemed too easy to believe. I had come across several of these kinds of puzzles in the various competitions I had entered over the years. They were even popular brain teasers in the puzzle workbooks I liked to fill out on the long plane rides Dad and I took to get to new dig site locations.

"It wants me to input the two missing numbers in the sequence," I explained. "By the looks of it, all we have to do is double the first number, then subtract one to get the next number. Then we double that number and subtract two. Then double that one, subtract three—"

"Yes, yes, we get it, so go on and place the tiles!" Monet urged, getting impatient. All the while, the Rose de France seemed to glow a little brighter.

I sifted through the pile of numbered tiles and found the ones I needed. Then I slid them into place to complete the number sequence:

$$3\ 5\ 8\ 13\ 22\ 39\ 72\ 137$$

With the last tile in place, there was a loud click, and the stone wall cracked open on one side, creating a door. Monet was the first to push through.

"This is it, Harley," Veronica whispered, consulting her map. "Only one more puzzle before the hidden chamber."

We took a short walk down a sloping tunnel and came to another wall. But this one had a massive metal door built into it, with the symbol of the Rose de France adorning the top and intricate carvings of dancing skeletons etched below it.

And below those carvings was a cryptogram.

My heart sank. Even though I loved trying to solve them, cryptograms were the types of puzzles I still needed the most practice with.

And I wasn't just solving this one to pass some time on an airplane. This time, my life depended on it.

"What do you need to do for this one?" Veronica asked.

"It's a cryptogram. That means there's some kind of phrase to figure out, but the words for that phrase are encrypted. So first, I have to find the cipher that will tell us what each letter in the sentence is *really* supposed to be. Then, I just need to put them all in the right places."

But this cryptogram was long. Really long. Longer than any I had ever attempted before:

```
_ _ _ _   _ _ _   _ _ _ ,
B N I Z   I Z X   D X H

_ _ _ _ _   _ _ _
X J I X G   H L E

_ _ _   _ _ _ _ _   _ _ _
B Z L   Z X V G V   V J O

_ _ _ _   _ _ _   _ _ _ _ _
Z V T X   I Z X   T L N F X Q

_ _   _ _ _ _ _   _ _ _ _ _
L S   I Z L Q X   R V Q Q X O
```

"And where do you find this cipher?" Veronica asked.

"That's the tricky part," I admitted. I started looking around the tunnel we were in. Surely, the cipher had to be hiding somewhere.

"We need a cipher," I called to the rest of our group. "Look for anything you can find carved into the wall."

The five of us fanned out across the tunnel, turning our lights up and down the wall.

It took a while, but we finally found something seemingly useful hiding on the back of the stone door we had come through at the other end of the tunnel. But all this carving read was:

AV EX IN OL UE

It *had* to be the cipher! But by the looks of it, it was only a partial cipher. Meaning it was up to me to figure out what the rest of the letters in the phrase were.

Think Harley, think! I told myself. *Preserve. Protect. Persevere* also echoed through my brain. Man, I'd never realized how many P's were in S.M.A.L.L.'s motto. Not to mention E's, too.

And that's when I realized what I was looking at.

"This cipher is for the vowels in the phrase!" I told Veronica, who had been trying to help me figure out what these letters could possibly mean. "A is really V. E is really X. I is really N—"

"And O is L, while U is E!" Veronica finished. "Yes, I see what you mean!"

From there, it was just a matter of plugging those few letters in and playing around with the words until we got a sentence with all the right letters that seemed to make sense. To my surprise, the phrase was in English.

WITH THE KEY, ENTER YOU WHO HEAR AND HAVE THE VOICES OF THOSE PASSED.

When the last letter had been placed, the big, metal door groaned deeply. But it didn't open. Instead, a cutout in the center of the door slid open, revealing a space just big enough for something small and round to be inserted.

"Step aside," Monet growled from behind us. "You two have played your part."

Monet pulled Veronica's stone pendant from his pocket. It was glowing just as brightly as the Rose de France.

"I cannot let you do this!" Veronica yelled out, leaping for Monet and the key. But his henchmen were too quick. One of them snatched her in mid-jump, and the other grabbed me firmly by the arm.

"Foolish girl," Monet mocked Veronica. "You will be the first person I set my army of bones upon. Then will come the rest of the ancient families of France."

He cackled wickedly as he inserted the pendant into the small opening in the door. The stone burst with bright purple light as the Rose de France did the same.

Then the door creaked and swung open. Monet stepped inside.

As I stood staring after him, I felt my heart sink into my stomach. Monet had reached the chamber.

We had failed.

CHAPTER 21
THE HIDDEN CHAMBER

"He's going to perform the ritual and wake the bones!" Veronica yelled out, struggling against Monet's bodyguard. "We have to do something!"

But we were no match for the henchmen. They just stood there, holding us firm, not even blinking. Didn't these guys care that the world as we knew it was about to end?

I could feel the tears began to creep out the sides of my eyes. I had failed S.M.A.L.L., my friend, my dad, and the people of Paris. Veronica and I had helped Monet reach the chamber in the hopes that we could stop him once we made it there. But that moment had come and gone.

What are we going to do now?

Several agonizing minutes passed. No noise came from the room Monet had just entered.

No cracking of stone, no bones coming to life. Nothing. The damp air from the tunnels was beginning to creep under my clothes. My knees were shaking.

A few more minutes passed and Monet bellowed out, "IT'S NOT WORKING!"

He sounded really mad. Which was saying something, considering he'd been pretty grumpy just about this entire time.

He stormed back through the door, his chubby cheeks red with fury. "I have found the chamber. I have the key and the Rose de France. And I have just added a drop of blood to the pedestal and placed the stone on top. So why is nothing happening?!"

He looked back and forth between Veronica and me like we might have the answers.

I sure didn't.

But Veronica was distracted. She was looking around the tunnel again with that strange expression on her face. The one she kept making every time she thought she heard voices.

And then it dawned on me.

"The cryptogram," I said. "The cryptogram is the answer."

"What do you mean?" Monet continued yelling.

"Veronica, don't you get it?" I asked her directly.

She looked at me, her wide eyes afraid. But she just shook her head.

"*With the key, enter you who hear and have the voices of those passed,*" I recited the cryptogram we had just solved. "You've been the protector of the key. You've been hearing voices ever since we came down into the Catacombs. And you have the voices of those passed because you do everything you can to protect the history of the families of France," I explained. "That means Monet isn't the person who can wake the bones with his ancient bloodline. You are."

I watched Veronica's eyes light up as she finally understood what I was saying.

"Impossible," Monet growled, his face getting red again. "This cannot be! My family is the most famous in France!"

He snapped his fingers and headed back through the metal door. His henchmen dragged us through right behind him.

The chamber of the Rose de France was massive. Sparkling white and gray stones had been used to build the walls, which towered up into a domed ceiling. Old, faded gravestones also lined the walls, noting where ancient elders had been laid to rest long ago. And across the room from us was a short stone staircase leading to an entryway blocked by a huge round boulder. It was the only other way out of the room.

The Rose de France sat in the middle of the chamber on a small pedestal, shimmering with purple light. But Monet was right—nothing else had seemed to happen while he was in here.

At least there weren't any bones walking around that I could see.

"I refuse to perform the ritual," Veronica said as the henchmen walked us to the center of the room. "And there is nothing you can do to make me," she told Monet.

He towered over her menacingly. "You will perform the ritual," he said, "or I will smash the Rose de France to pieces and take all of Paris down with it."

What were we supposed to do now? Sacrifice the world, or sacrifice the city of Paris?

There was no winning in this situation. Either option was a terrible idea.

I bit my lip hard and pored over everything we knew up to this point. We had solved every riddle and clue to make it to this moment. But it was Veronica who must make the final choice. I wasn't sure what Monet would do to us, but we couldn't let him win.

I looked to Veronica. She nodded. We both knew what was right. For the people of Paris. For our families. For S.M.A.L.L.

"Do what you must," Veronica told Monet. "But I will not utter a single word of your ritual to bring the bones to life."

Monet's goatee twitched angrily as he glared at the two of us. "Very well," he snarled, picking up the precious stone. "Then you leave me no choice." He raised the glowing stone above his head, ready to smash it onto the hard floor.

Just then, the room began to vibrate.

The giant stone boulder blocking the main entrance made a terrible sound, like a giant grinding his teeth together while he sleeps. The boulder shuddered and began to move. Rolling away from its location and into the chamber.

"How is this possible?" Monet said breathlessly, the Rose de France still above his head.

His question was answered by an echoing bark. A bark that I knew all too well.

"Daisy!" I yelled out.

She came bounding through the doorway and down the stone steps, sprinting right for us. Behind her, Mario Costa also ducked through the doorway.

Monet (and the rest of us, to be honest) were completely stunned. "You are too late, Mario!" he yelled furiously at him. "And now you will perish!"

He hurled the Rose de France toward the floor.

But Daisy was too quick for him.

She leaped for Monet as the stone came down, snatching it right out of the air with her mouth. She skidded across the floor, still holding her new ball, tail wagging happily.

"*Une chienne!*" Monet said for the second time that night, glaring at Daisy. "Give it back!"

But before he could chase her down, a dozen police officers streamed into the chamber behind Mario. The men who had been holding Veronica and me hostage dropped their hands and began to run back to the tunnels. The police quickly stopped them. Veronica and I melted into a puddle on the floor, relief hitting us like a tidal wave.

The sounds of Monet and his henchmen being handcuffed echoed down the hallways.

Daisy was licking my face with all her might. Veronica looked at me and smiled.

"Are you girls alright?" Mario was standing over us with a concerned look on his face. "Here, let me help you up."

We each took his hand and stood to our feet. The police brushed passed us with the trio of criminals in their possession. I felt a smile touch the corners of my lips.

We did it. The city of Paris had just been saved by a couple of young girls, a man who was afraid of his own shadow, and a little white dog who liked to play fetch.

CHAPTER 22
A BRIGHT NEW DAY

"You should have seen the look on his face when Daisy came running into the room!"

I was recounting our entire journey down into the Catacombs for Mario, who was more than eager to hear the story. He was a Catacombs explorer at heart, after all. After we visited him, he got the sense that something very wrong would be happening down in the Catacombs soon. Since he'd made his way to the stone boulder blocking the main entrance to the Rose de France chamber once before, he figured he could find his way there again. And this time, he would bring some police officers with him.

Meeting Daisy along the way was just a happy coincidence.

"But how did you get the stone door to open?" Veronica asked him. I had been wondering the exact same thing.

Mario shrugged. "I think because the Rose de France was already inside the room, the door would open for anyone. Daisy and I simply walked up, and it started to move."

Thank goodness for that.

We were all safely above ground now, watching the sun just

starting to rise over Paris. Monet and his henchmen had been carted off by the police, which meant Veronica had finally been able to perform the *other* ritual. The one that would keep the bones of the Catacombs at peace forever.

"I told you not to get involved with Albert Monet, did I not?" Mario asked now, trying to stifle a smirk. "The Catacombs are no place for children. Or adults, for that matter."

"Does that mean your exploring days are over?" I asked him.

He nodded. "Yes, I believe so. But that also means I can now live other parts of my life. Other parts that I have not lived for far too long." He smiled at Veronica and me. "Thank you for that."

"Harley James, what on *Earth* have you gotten yourself into this time?" an angry voice said from behind me. It was another kind of bark I knew all too well.

I turned around. "Dad?" Sure enough, there he was, wearing his field clothes and boots, which were all covered in smudges of dirt. "I thought you went back to the dig," I said.

"I did! But when I didn't hear from you all day, and then you didn't answer any of my calls or texts all night…well, I got worried. Which I know I'm not supposed to do anymore, but I can't help it. I'm sorry."

I was so glad to see him that I threw myself at him in the biggest bear hug I could manage. "No, Dad, I'm sorry. I didn't mean what I said. I love having you around," I told him.

He hugged me back. "I'm overprotective of you because I love you so much, Cat-Cat. You know that, right?" he asked, pulling me in front of him. His eyes didn't look sad anymore. "But I'll work on finding a balance between being protective and annoying, okay?"

I nodded and laughed. "And I'll work on finding a balance between exercising independence and getting myself into heaps of trouble."

Now he was laughing. "Deal," he said.

Behind me, Veronica cleared her throat loudly.

"Give me a minute to say goodbye to my friend, Dad. Then I promise I'll fill you in," I told him. He nodded and went to introduce himself to Mario. I had a hunch they'd find each other endlessly fascinating.

"You called me your friend," Veronica said.

"Of course I did. After the ordeal we just went through together, I think we're more than just fellow agents of S.M.A.L.L."

Veronica smiled. "Agreed. I am happy to have a friend like you, Harley James." She stuck her hand out for a shake, but I pulled her into a hug instead. Guess I was feeling particularly warm and fuzzy toward people at the moment.

"So, what will you do now?" I asked her as we parted. "Y'know, since the Catacombs are safe. And so is Paris, for that matter."

Veronica shrugged. "This city is filled with ancient artifacts. I'm sure S.M.A.L.L. will have another job for me in no time," she said. "How about you?"

I glanced over her shoulder at my dad, who was still talking with Mario.

"Hard to say where my dad's next dig will take us. But wherever it is, I plan to get in a little less trouble than I did in Paris."

Veronica laughed. "That can be difficult when your job is to *Preserve. Protect. Persevere.*"

If I only knew how right that statement would prove to be.

ABOUT THE AUTHOR

Leah Cupps is an author, designer, entrepreneur, and self-proclaimed bookworm. She conceptualized the Harley James series with her oldest daughter, Savannah, who had developed an interest in Mayan history.

The mother & daughter duo worked together to create a new world, which became the foundation for the first Harley James series.

Leah resides in Indiana with her husband and three children. She is also the co-founder of the small family-owned publishing company Vision Forty Press.

Did you like this book and want to help spread the word?
It would mean a lot to me if you would leave a short review online. Every review helps with visibility and allows me to write more books.
Thank you,
Leah Cupps

READY FOR THE NEXT ADVENTURE TO BEGIN?

Book 1: Harley James & the Mystery of the Mayan Kings

Will Harley find the missing Mayan statue in time to save world? Join Harley and her friends as they explore temples, escape tombs and fight off some snakes in the original Harley James adventure!

ORDER NOW AT AMAZON.COM

Book 2: Harley James & the Peril of the Pirates Curse

Join Harley and her friends as they swashbuckle their way through the mysteries of Port Royal, Jamaica—the famouse sunken pirate city of the Carribbean!

ORDER NOW AT AMAZON.COM

Made in the USA
Monee, IL
02 July 2023